MONEY with Jess

MONEY *with* *Jess*

YOUR ULTIMATE GUIDE to HOUSEHOLD BUDGETING

JESSICA IRVINE

WILEY

First published in 2022 by John Wiley & Sons Australia, Ltd

42 McDougall St, Milton Qld 4064
Office also in Melbourne

Typeset in Bembo Std 12pt/16pt

ISBN: 978-0-730-39823-3

A catalogue record for this
book is available from the
National Library of Australia

Cover design by Wiley
Author photos: © Louie Douvis
Cover background image: © silverpak/Shutterstock
Title hand lettering image: © very-very/Shutterstock
Lightbulb image: © Dashk/stock.adobe.com
Arrow image and notebook image: © Anatoliy Babiy/iStock
Highlighter image: © OpenClipart-Vectors from Pixabay.

Disclaimer
The material in this publication is of the nature of general comment only, and does not represent professional advice. It is not intended to provide specific guidance for particular circumstances and it should not be relied on as the basis for any decision to take action or not take action on any matter which it covers. Readers should obtain professional advice where appropriate, before making any such decision. To the maximum extent permitted by law, the author and publisher disclaim all responsibility and liability to any person, arising directly or indirectly from any person taking or not taking action based on the information in this publication.

Proudly Printed in Australia by Ligare Book Printers.

How to get immediate help

If you are in financial distress, call the National Debt Helpline on 1800 007 007 on weekdays between 9.30 am and 4.30 pm (Australia only).

An army of trained financial counsellors is standing by to help you negotiate with creditors (people you owe money to) and to help get you back on financial track.

It's a completely free, independent and confidential service funded by the government and delivered by not-for-profit organisations in your state.

You can also access a 'live chat' feature on their website: ndh.org.au.

How to access my free resources

Throughout this book, I refer to many worksheets I have created to help you get started on your budgeting journey. All the resources I refer to are available to download for free from my website: jessicairvine.com.au.

Check it out and get downloading today!

For Henry xx

Contents

Introduction

Hello friends!

My name is Jess and I'm good at money. Like, really good.

It's taken a long time for me to be able to say that with confidence—partly because it wasn't always true.

Shortly after I divorced in my mid-30s, a colleague suggested I write a book titled *A Man Is Not a Financial Plan* about how to manage your finances as a single parent. Trouble was, I didn't know how.

Which is a bit embarrassing, really, given I've now been working as a high-profile economics and finance journalist for some of Australia's most prestigious newspapers for the better part of two decades.

I have a university degree in economics and philosophy. It's my job to regularly pass judgement on how the nation's treasurer is managing the country's budget. I've reported on 18 annual federal budgets so far (not counting the 'bonus' emergency budgets and stimulus packages during the Global Financial Crisis and COVID-19).

I've interviewed prime ministers on live TV, enjoyed private one-on-one lunches with Reserve Bank governors and I regularly text and speak with treasury secretaries, both past and present.

'I've been to budgeting nerd paradise'—as the 1970s chanteuse Charlene once famously (almost) sang—but I'd never, until quite recently, taken a very serious look at my own personal finances.

It's not that I was ever particularly bad at money, depending on your definition of this. I've never had a credit card I couldn't pay off in full each month to avoid paying interest. And I've always paid my bills on time.

But, wow, have I spent a lot of money during my 40 years on this earth!

As my career blossomed in my late 20s and early 30s, I thought nothing of dropping $400 on a new designer suit jacket, a meal at a posh restaurant or a night at a fancy hotel.

I remember spending about that much to have my childhood copy of *The Lord of the Rings* rebound in an expensive, fabric-clad hard cover by a specialist antique book store.

Pretty cool, right?

But then, one day, you find yourself pushing 40 as a divorced single mum who doesn't own a home, has never invested in shares or property and has no idea if she's on course for a comfortable retirement.

I'm the classic example of someone who knows a lot about something in theory, but was pretty crap at applying it in practice.

Looking back, I can see that at the time of my colleague's book-writing suggestion, I was still drowning in deep shame and sadness at the failure of my marriage and my single parenthood.

But, as the dust began to settle on my new life, I did start to slowly pick myself up and put my financial life together—perhaps for the first time.

I bought my first home as a single mum aged 38 (I share all my best hacks for navigating that gruelling process in chapter 6—stay tuned!).

At about that time, I began writing a weekly personal finance column for the 'Money' sections of the *Sunday Age* and *Sun Herald* newspapers.

In it, I finally began applying all the economic theory I had learned to overhauling my real-life finances—and sharing all the gory details with readers.

My Instagram account, @moneywithjess, began to grow rapidly and I pitched the idea of a weekly email newsletter of the same name—Money with Jess—to share the results of my one-woman mission to budget, save and invest.

You name a crazy money-saving experiment, I've tried it!

I once kept a spreadsheet to calculate the precise cost of every meal I cooked for one week to figure out a realistic food budget (it worked out about $85 per week for me and my son). I used another spreadsheet to tally the cost of buying the same basket of groceries from two different supermarkets to find out which was cheaper (spoiler alert: Aldi).

I kept a handwritten tally on a sticky note stuck to a bottle of dishwashing powder to figure out the per-wash cost and whether it is cheaper than using tablets (it is, mostly because you can just use less detergent).

I didn't buy any clothes for an entire year. I cut my own hair. I gave up getting blonde foils (you can just see the remnant of my former colour on the tips of my hair in the cover photo for this book).

I began meticulously tracking my spending and in one article published the details of every single dollar I spent in one financial year (I know you'll want to know: it was $88 379.84 in 2020–21).

Bigger picture: I embarked on an epic hunt for the best mortgage deal, locking in my interest rate in for two years at 1.84 per cent and scoring a $4000 'cash back' for my efforts.

I began making regular voluntary contributions to my retirement savings account.

And finally, in May 2021, I did something I had never previously dreamed of. I began investing directly in the share market for the first time—something I continue to do on a regular monthly basis and will tell you about in chapter 10.

How I found financial freedom

Underpinning all my progress, I believe, is a budgeting system I created to sort, organise and track my money: the system this book is ultimately designed to teach you to use yourself.

I've divided this book into three parts that roughly correlate to the personal journey I've been on with my money.

Part I is all about getting you in the right 'money mindset' to succeed. I share some of the details of my own therapy journey, where I learned about the critical role of emotions and thoughts in ultimately driving your behaviours and outcomes. Getting into a healthy 'money mindset' requires ridding yourself of some unhelpful beliefs you've probably picked up about money, namely that it's too boring or too complex. To assist, I've outlined seven 'money myths' you'll need to ditch.

In part II, we put together an annual budget to show you where your money is going. Whether it's planning for retirement, applying for a loan or deciding what size emergency fund you need, having an idea of your individual spending is critical.

When I first attempted to do this for myself, I quickly realised how useful it would be to have a comprehensive checklist to work through of all the things people can spend money on.

Being the self-confessed 'numbers nerd' that I am, I began trawling through statistical surveys of household expenditure from Australia and other advanced nations—a search that would lead me all the way to the United Nations—to find the ultimate budget categories system.

None suited my purposes, however. So I decided to create my own. In chapter 6, I run you through what I believe to be a complete checklist of all the purchases you will ever make in life, sorted neatly into my unique 10 budget categories.

Dog treats, garden hoses, charity donations—I know where they all go! I truly believe I have identified every possible expense you need to consider when putting together a household budget. I found the process so satisfying and I hope you do too.

Of course, once you begin to become aware of where all your money is going, you'll want to begin trimming and saving where you can. So I've sprinkled part II of this book with over 300 money-saving hacks to help you (you'll find them in green boxes throughout). You're so welcome!

Finally, part III of this book is all about the system I personally use to regularly budget and track my money. It contains information about how to access and use all my free, downloadable resources, including my Annual Budget worksheet, Spending Tracker, Monthly Budget worksheet and Future Fund worksheet. I am regularly asked to explain how they all work, so this has been my chance to explain in full!

Why I wrote this book

My deepest desire is that the information you're about to read will help alleviate some of the suffering so many people feel when they think about money. Undeniably, many people suffer real, actual financial deprivation, unable to make ends meet on meagre incomes, with severe repercussions for their mental and even physical health and wellbeing.

But I'm also talking about a different kind of suffering—one that is perhaps even more widespread.

It's the suffering people endure when they simply don't feel in control of the money they do have; when they lack the confidence to make empowered decisions about money on a daily basis, let alone save for their future selves.

Studies have shown that, beyond a certain point, a person's level of income is a much less important driver of their wellbeing than the sense that they have of being in control of their financial situation.

For two decades, the authors of the Australian Unity Wellbeing Index survey have asked Australians to rate, on a scale of 1 to 10, how satisfied they are with their life. Their clear conclusion is that it's not money, per se, but 'financial control' that matters most. 'People with lower income can actually achieve higher wellbeing than those on higher incomes, so long as they have a higher perceived control over their financial position', the study authors conclude.

Indeed, financial control forms one part of a 'golden triangle of happiness' that predominantly determines our wellbeing, alongside 'personal relationships' and a 'sense of purpose'.

As I sit down to write this introduction, I feel quite emotional at how far I've come. And because I'm a big fan of giving precise labels to emotions—as you'll soon discover—specifically, I feel proud, hopeful and optimistic for both myself and for you, as you embark on your own budgeting journey.

From a place of fear and despair, I have arrived at a sense of calm and joy when it comes to managing my money.

On a daily basis, I spend my money with confidence, and in ways that align with my own personal values and desires. When I say 'yes' to spending, it's a 'hell yes'. I cherish the things I buy because I have done the inner work to know what really does—or does not—bring me pleasure. And I don't waste money on the latter.

It is my deepest desire to share with you the same sense of peace and calm I now feel when I look at my finances. I want you to know it's possible to have a happier and more stress-free relationship with your money.

One last thing before we begin.

I'd like to take a moment to acknowledge what I feel is an elephant in the room.

You've seen the cover of this book. I don't look like your typical personal finance expert. I'm not particularly old. And I'm not a man (although, if you want to see a fun picture of what that would look like, you can quickly flick to page 35). I think it's useful to share that writing this book has been one of the greatest challenges of my life. In addition to the usual struggles of writing a book, I've faced an uphill battle against 'imposter syndrome': an uncomfortable feeling of 'Who am I to be telling people what to do with their money?'

Despite almost two decades of writing about economics and finance, I have still, at times, struggled internally to picture myself as a person who can and should sit down and write an authoritative book about money—one that both men and women can benefit from reading. It's hard to be what you don't often see.

Because, unlike my colleague's original suggestion, this is not a book aimed specifically at women. Yes, I am a woman. And yes, ladies, that retirement savings gap is very real. And yes, as it turns out, a man is not a financial plan.

But I hate the way personal finance books and advice are universally clad in 'pink' to target women and 'blue' for men (something my publisher can affirm, after all the grief I gave over wanting a 'gender-neutral' cover and design for this book: 'Too girly; try again!' was my repeated refrain).

If you've got a head and a heart, and some money to manage, you will benefit from reading this book. It's taken me considerable internal effort to arrive at a place where I can say that with confidence. But it's true. So, I'll say it again:

My name is Jess and I'm good at money. Bloody good, in fact.

And you can be, too.

I know, because I'm about to show you how.

Let's get started, shall we?

PART I
How to build a healthy money mindset

Before we get to the action parts of this book, where we organise your money and figure out where you want it to go, we need to stop for a hot minute and figure out how you currently think and feel about money.

In my career as a finance journalist, I've observed the way lots of people—such as readers, editors, fellow journalists, politicians and voters—think about money.

Overwhelmingly, I see people stuck in a pattern of thinking money is just too complex—too overwhelming—to understand. It's also common to believe that money is boring (this one hurts my soul!) or that it's just the case that some people suck at money.

The good news is that if you're one of those people who believe these things, honey, you're wrong. Don't feel too bad about it. An entire financial system exists that profits from your overwhelm. To fight it, you need to learn to manage your thoughts and emotions about money, which is what we're about to do now.

Perhaps some of us pop out of the womb knowing how to make good money decisions. But, believe me, most of us don't. The ability to manage money is a skillset that needs to be learned.

Unfortunately, many of us miss the memo and by the time we're old enough to control our money, we're already trapped in a toxic relationship with it.

We turn a blind eye to our overall financial position. We spend up big to calm our inner storms. We stick our heads in the sand and just hope our money problems will figure themselves out, one day. So much mental distress is caused this way and so much of it could be avoided, I believe, if we just took some time to really stare our money in the face. That's what this whole book is about.

But before we start looking at your personal money situation, I want to spend part I of this book really getting to the bottom of all the unhealthy attitudes towards money you may have unconsciously internalised—and then to help liberate you from them.

I'll teach you how to become a mini emotions detective, able to root out all the feelings you feel when you think about money. We'll then trace the origin of these emotions back to the thoughts you're having about money. And then, we'll replace those old thoughts with some more helpful ones.

Be warned: it might take some time and effort to really rid yourself of these unhelpful beliefs about money. But you'll feel so much better when you do, I promise!

It's never too late to start reframing your thoughts and feelings around money. So let's get into it.

1

Identifying your money emotions

I want you to start by really focusing on that word for a moment: MONEY.

Say it out loud with me: 'MONEY'.

Or, if you're in a public place (and you haven't already embarrassed yourself), just really stare at that word on the page for moment: MONEY.

What emotion do you feel in your body when you see that word or hear it spoken?

MONEY

MONEY

MONEY

Don't worry. If you're anything like I was, you may struggle with this exercise.

I've been seeing a psychologist on and off for about half a decade now. These days, I usually enjoy our sessions — they're like a workout for my brain.

Most of my very early sessions, however, consisted of my kindly therapist bookending everything I said with the question, 'And how did that make you feel?' and me just shuffling uncomfortably in my seat and staring back somewhat blankly.

After one particularly difficult session, that dreaded question came up again: 'How did that make you feel, Jess?'

'Analytical', I replied, adding, 'Is analytical a feeling?'

'No, Jess', came the reply, 'analytical is pretty much the opposite of a feeling'.

Oh.

It wasn't until one day when my therapist actually provided me with a potentially relevant word to describe my emotion that I began to connect the dots.

Truth is, unless you've been taught how, it can be difficult to recognise what emotion, or what combination of emotions (there can be many!) you are feeling at any point in time.

Yet it is so very important. Because emotions drive our behaviours; and it's our behaviours that produce our outcomes.

Now, I can almost hear you thinking, 'But Jess, I am a very evolved person. I always put reason ahead of passion. I am not driven by my emotions!'

To which I say, 'Bless you, dear reader. Yes, you are. You just don't realise it—yet'.

Despite our protestations to the contrary, so many of us these days exist in a perpetual state of emotional arousal. I used to have just one blanket word to describe how I was feeling: 'stressed'.

When you are 'stressed' you spend quite a bit of time—and money—running around trying to distract yourself from that sensation with alcohol, comfort food, internet dating—or whatever your distraction of choice is. Been there, tried that.

The emotions wheel

Until you do the work to identify and label the root emotions you are actually feeling—sadness, fear, loneliness—you're really just running on a treadmill (and not the good kind that gets you fit!).

I don't think I deliberately set out to suppress my emotions. Well, not entirely. I think I just genuinely lacked a sufficiently rich vocabulary to describe the feelings I was experiencing in my body.

Realising this, my therapist quickly supplied me with a so-called 'feelings wheel' or 'emotions wheel' to help me when I got stuck.

There are lots of different versions of this on the internet, the origin of which is contested. On the next page you will find one version that I like.

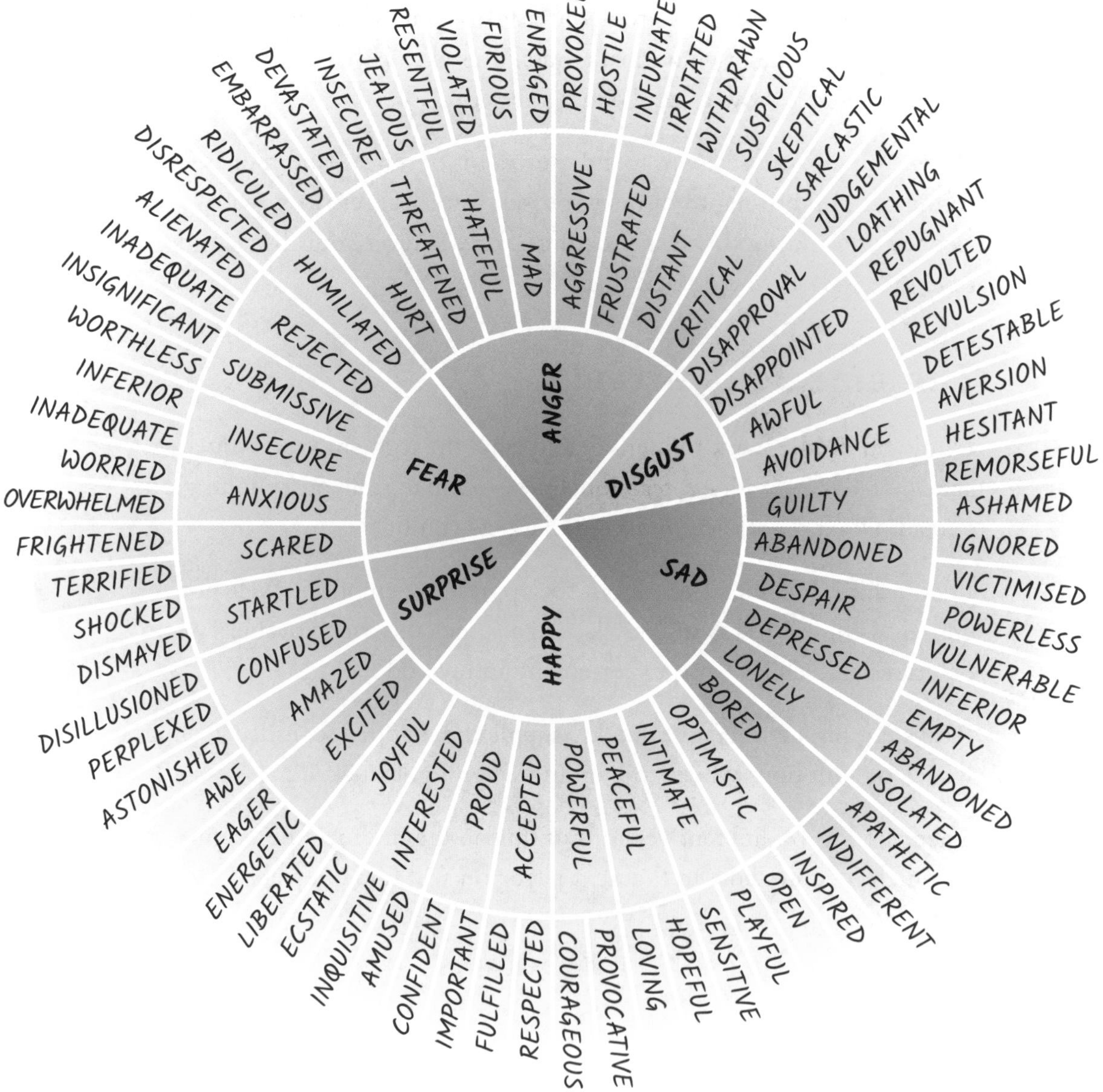
ANGER
DISGUST
SAD
HAPPY
SURPRISE
FEAR
MAD
AGGRESSIVE
FRUSTRATED
DISTANT
CRITICAL
DISAPPROVAL
DISAPPOINTED
AWFUL
AVOIDANCE
GUILTY
ABANDONED
DESPAIR
DEPRESSED
LONELY
BORED
OPTIMISTIC
INTIMATE
PEACEFUL
POWERFUL
ACCEPTED
PROUD
INTERESTED
JOYFUL
EXCITED
AMAZED
CONFUSED
STARTLED
SCARED
ANXIOUS
INSECURE
SUBMISSIVE
REJECTED
HUMILIATED
HURT
THREATENED
HATEFUL
ENRAGED
PROVOKED
HOSTILE
INFURIATED
IRRITATED
WITHDRAWN
SUSPICIOUS
SKEPTICAL
SARCASTIC
JUDGEMENTAL
LOATHING
REPUGNANT
REVOLTED
REVULSION
DETESTABLE
AVERSION
HESITANT
REMORSEFUL
ASHAMED
IGNORED
VICTIMISED
POWERLESS
VULNERABLE
INFERIOR
EMPTY
ABANDONED
ISOLATED
APATHETIC
INDIFFERENT
INSPIRED
OPEN
PLAYFUL
SENSITIVE
HOPEFUL
LOVING
PROVOCATIVE
COURAGEOUS
RESPECTED
FULFILLED
IMPORTANT
CONFIDENT
AMUSED
INQUISITIVE
ECSTATIC
LIBERATED
ENERGETIC
EAGER
AWE
ASTONISHED
PERPLEXED
DISILLUSIONED
DISMAYED
SHOCKED
TERRIFIED
FRIGHTENED
OVERWHELMED
WORRIED
INADEQUATE
INFERIOR
WORTHLESS
INSIGNIFICANT
INADEQUATE
ALIENATED
DISRESPECTED
RIDICULED
EMBARRASSED
DEVASTATED
INSECURE
JEALOUS
RESENTFUL
VIOLATED
FURIOUS

As you can see, in the centre of the wheel sit six core human emotional states: happy, sad, disgust, anger, fear and surprise. Psychologists disagree about which ones should occupy the central space, but these will do for our purposes.

Fanning out from the centre, you see ever more nuanced words to describe subsets of the core emotions. Let your eye roam over the middle and outer circles for a moment. Do you just feel sad? Or do you also feel despair or powerless? Do you feel just fearful, or also anxious and overwhelmed?

The reality is, you can feel multiple emotions, from different slices of the wheel, all at the same time.

These days, I keep a wheel just like this plastered in the front of every journal I write in. I refer to it regularly to help me identify my emotional state. I sometimes make it a personal challenge to name as many relevant emotions as I can!

I have found this simple act of naming my emotions to be an incredibly powerful tool for helping to dissipate the very emotions I'm feeling.

'But Jess, what's all this got to do with money? I've read several pages of your book now and I still don't *feel* rich. What gives?'

Okay, let me come to the point.

I want you to now look at the emotions wheel and identify exactly which words apply to you when you think about *money*—either your own personal financial circumstances or the notion of money in general. You can circle the words on the page, or write a list in a separate notebook. Try not to judge yourself—nobody is watching. Just try to name as many relevant emotions as you can.

Here are a few of the very common ones people gravitate to:

- **scared**
- **overwhelmed**
- **anxious**
- **worried**
- **aversion**
- **ashamed**
- **powerless**
- **despair**
- **guilty**
- **judgemental**
- **hesitant**
- **apathetic**
- **inferior.**

In your body, you might feel some of these emotions as a tightness in your chest, a clenched jawline or hunched shoulders.

If that's you, take another moment right now to just breathe for a second. Go on. Deep breath in … and out.

Relax your shoulders away from your ears; now your jaw, letting your tongue drop away from the roof your mouth.

There, isn't that better?

Go on, take another deep breath on me. They're completely free, I promise.

Now I want you to know that all these feelings you feel about money are very common and very normal. I have felt them too.

But what if I told you there was also another way to feel about money?

What if I told you it is possible, instead, to feel peaceful, hopeful, optimistic, courageous, confident, proud and liberated?

Sound too good to be true?

It's not. These are words I now feel when I think about money. I know others feel them too.

It turns out we can alter the emotions we feel about something. And in chapter 2, we're going to work through transforming the emotions you feel about your money.

But we have to do some more detective work first.

Where do emotions come from?

You see, emotions don't just arise out of nowhere. They are the body's and mind's reaction to the world around us *and*—even more explicitly—the thoughts and beliefs that we have about that world.

These can be thoughts you aren't even consciously aware of; they're just thoughts swimming in the social soup you've been fed all your life from society, governments, media, your family and friends.

Often we're not even aware we're having a specific thought. Sometimes, we're just having so many thoughts in such rapid succession, it's too hard to pinpoint one in particular.

But I promise you, if you are having a strong emotion, it is being driven by a thought you are also having.

Luckily, there is an ingenious way to identify thoughts and distinguish them from emotions.

Emotions can be summarised in one word—for example, 'fear', 'joy' or 'sadness'.

Thoughts, by contrast, come in sentence form—for example, 'I am going to fail the test'; 'Nobody likes me'; 'I will never be able to own a home'.

Logic decrees that there can only be so many words to describe emotions, which is why it's often easier to try identifying them before thoughts.

Thoughts—comprising of a string of words—exist in almost infinitely more variety, so catching yourself in the process of having a specific thought can be very difficult. But necessary if you want to be able to choose to think another thought that could, in turn, drive a different—perhaps more pleasurable—emotional state.

Because here's the thing. Thoughts are not facts.

They certainly can be. 'I think the sky is blue' is both a thought and a fact. But 'I think my friend didn't text me back because they don't like me and I am a worthless person'—while certainly a thought you could have—is not a fact.

Why is that not a fact? Well, first, because no human is worthless. But also because it could just as easily be the case that your friend not texting you back, in fact, had nothing to do with you. They lost their phone. They are in a meeting. Or they simply don't have the mental capacity to reply.

What we choose to think about a given situation matters because the emotional state it creates will, ultimately, drive our actual behaviour.

If you feel scared, you will likely run away, if possible.

If you feel guilty, you will seek to hide.

If you feel rejected, you might sit on the couch all night ordering Uber Eats.

Here is a helpful chart I made to summarise this thought-emotion-behaviour chain of causation.

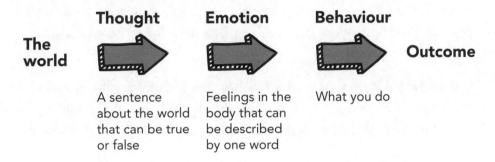

The world

Thought → A sentence about the world that can be true or false

Emotion → Feelings in the body that can be described by one word

Behaviour → What you do

Outcome

Now let's apply it to the real-world scenario of a friend not texting you back.

If your *thought* is that they didn't text because they don't like you, this might lead you to *feel* a combination of sadness, inferiority and rejection. It might lead you to the *behaviour* of withdrawing from your friend, or sending them a series of disgruntled and hostile messages demanding they explain themselves. Outcome? That friendship may disintegrate.

But what if you chose a different thought? What if you chose the *thought* that your friend is probably overwhelmed by something else in their life and that they will respond when they can. You might *feel* disappointed, but you might also feel peaceful and loving towards your friend. The *behaviour* this drives might be to simply give them the space they need, or maybe to follow up later with a brief message expressing your hope that they are well. Outcome? You may very well deepen or cultivate your friendship further.

Critically, by carefully selecting your thought in this example, you can not only avoid a distressing emotional state yourself, but also better the outcomes in your life.

Being able to identify both your emotions and underlying thoughts — and ultimately choose more accurate or helpful thoughts — is an invaluable life skill and one we are not often taught in school. It takes practice. If you can afford it, I highly recommend doing this work with a trained professional.

But you've paid good money for this book on the promise it will make you better at money, so let me do some of the hard 'thought identifying' work for you — at least when it comes to your relationship with money.

For those of you whose emotional response is to feel fear, powerlessness or apathy about money, I have some good news!

The thoughts you are having about money are very likely false. It is possible for you to think new and better thoughts about money.

In chapter 2, I debunk seven of the most common money myths I've encountered. I also lay out seven new thoughts about money for you to consider.

Not only do I think these new thoughts will be more helpful to you, I also happen to believe they are true.

Now isn't that a nice thought?

Let's go.

2

Seven money thoughts you need to ditch right now

Yippee! This is the part where I tell you how to manifest a Porsche simply by using the power of your mind and positive thinking, right?

Well, no. If I knew how to do that, I would have manifested one by now and driven off into the sunset.

No, I can't tell you how to think yourself into owning a Porsche overnight. But maybe—just maybe—I can get you thinking some more positive thoughts about money, which in turn might prompt you to spend a little less than you earn, save a little and, you know, maybe one day rent a Porsche for a day.

Baby steps, people.

One thing I do know is that if you believe any of the following seven thoughts about money, you're unlikely to make much headway in getting on top of your finances.

It's time to drill into these core beliefs and dig out the decay. Then we'll fill in the gaps with a fresh set of money beliefs. Then, in parts II and III of this book I'll equip you with a new set of money habits to help you maintain good financial hygiene.

So here we go. Here are the seven most common money myths I see, along with seven better thoughts to replace them with so you can begin building a more healthy mindset around money.

Money myth #1
Money is too complex to understand

One of the most common beliefs I encounter about money is that it is very complex — too hard to ever really understand.

I actually make a pretty decent living out of this false belief by getting paid to explain topics such as interest rates, house prices and inflation.

And yes, things can start to get a little weird when you talk about cryptocurrencies, quantitative easing and secular stagnation.

But let me let you in on a little secret:

At its heart, money is dead simple.

Ultimately, money is just a medium for exchange. You give up your time and skills to your employer and, in exchange, they give you money. You then take this money and exchange it for all the goods and services you need and want to live a happy life.

There it is: money explained in a few easy sentences.

The nifty thing is, if you can learn to curb your spending desires over your lifetime, you can reduce your need to work as hard or for as long.

Alternatively, you can work harder and upskill to get more money to exchange for more of the things you want to buy. You get to choose.

Only problem is, across your lifespan you're likely to encounter periods of time when you're less able to exchange your time for money. You'll still need to buy stuff, of course, but you won't have the money coming in to fund it. Economists call this the 'life cycle hypothesis' and it necessitates a process known as 'consumption smoothing'.

When you're very young, it's likely your parents will spot you the difference, paying for your food and accommodation until you move out of home.

In early adulthood, when you're either studying or not earning much money, it's likely, however, that you will incur some debts in order to fund your income shortfall. Borrowing to fund your education or to travel can be a good decision if, over your lifespan, it broadens your horizons and boosts your future income-earning potential.

At some stage, however, you're going to have to pay for the stuff you bought and pay the debt back.

To do this, you need to keep earning money and start scoring some pay rises. This is the time to start thinking about both paying off your debts and starting to set a little extra money aside to support yourself in the future when you are older and either can't work, or don't want to work.

And that's really all there is to personal finance.

Many personal finance books get you to start out by dreaming up your individual 'money goals'. But I reckon there's really only one goal that people need, and that is to generate enough lifetime income to fund their lifetime wants and needs.

This means spending less than you earn during your working life and saving to help fund the spending needs and desires of your future caravan-hauling retired self (the version of you who gets to spend all the money—yay!).

Of course, you may decide to be more ambitious and accumulate savings to pass on to somebody else—like your children or a charity—to fund their future wants and needs. That's a choice you can make. But it's not necessary. Only one thing's certain: you can't take any money with you when you die.

So, if I had to summarise personal finance (for non-retired people) in just one sentence, it would be this:

Spend less than you earn; invest the rest.

It's a magic little formula that we'll get to in more detail in chapter 4.

'But Jess, can it really just be as simple as that?' I hear you asking.

Yes, it can. But it's no accident that you think otherwise.

A lot of people make a lot of money out of you feeling overwhelm and inertia when it comes to managing your money. Retailers sell you more products you don't really need. Banks and insurers sign you up to products and then charge you a 'loyalty tax', keeping their lowest prices for newer customers. Buy Now, Pay Later providers get you on the hook before you realise you could have just done 'Save Now, Spend Later' and skipped the late payment fees.

I do think it's true that young people are having to navigate a riskier and more uncertain financial landscape than their parents. Housing affordability is a bigger headache, student debts are higher and ultra-low interest rates have made the process of saving a deposit on a first home that much harder. Incomes are also more varied and insecure.

That being said, nothing has changed fundamentally about the common money goal all humans share: to exchange enough of your time to earn enough income to fund your present, past and future needs and wants.

Debunking money myth #1

OLD THOUGHT	NEW THOUGHT
Money is too complex to understand.	I get to choose how I earn, spend and invest my money, and that's all I really have to do.
OLD EMOTIONS	NEW EMOTIONS
Overwhelmed, worried, inadequate	Empowered, optimistic, ambitious
OLD BEHAVIOUR	NEW BEHAVIOUR
I avoid thinking about or seeing anything to do with money.	I seek out and engage with new information to learn more about money.

Money myth #2
Some people are just bad at money (and I'm one of them!)

Do you know the answer to 10 minus 8? Yes? Congratulations! You have all the essential skills you need to manage money.

The maths of money is pretty simple. Perhaps it's the effort and attention required to manage your money that you're missing—for now. But if you knew the following, maybe you'd try a little harder ...

It's a commonly held belief that some people are just born with a talent for something, and others just aren't. We think movie stars and sports stars are naturally gifted, and never imagine that we could cultivate such skills. Not true, according to the pioneering work of psychologist Carol Dweck. In her 2007 book *Mindset: The new psychology of success*, Dweck delved into all the ways seemingly talented people have, in fact, chosen to cultivate their skills over time through a lot of dedicated practice.

Dweck's work led to the more recent advice to parents that children should be praised for the effort they put in, not for their innate attributes: little Sally didn't do well on the test because she's 'clever', she did well because she studied hard. The trick is that one leads to the other: it is via our efforts that we become talented in a given field. It is through study that we become clever. Of course, physique and biology may play a role at the very top echelons of sport, but it is application and effort that get sports stars to the starting line to begin with.

Being good at money is no different.

You're sitting on the money game sidelines now, but with a little time and effort, you could be playing centre field. (Forgive me, I am crap at sporting analogies. Correction: I have not previously dedicated a lot of time to understanding sport, but with enough time and application, I could provide you with a better analogy — I am just presently choosing not to …).

If we dig a little deeper, we could also take solace from the fact that we are all — every one of us — a bit crap at money.

Why? Because we are human.

For a long time, economists liked to build their models of the world based on the assumption of a perfectly rational human called 'homo-economicus'. Homo-economicus was the perfect pleasure-seeking, decision-making machine. Presented with a set of choices, he (yes, it was usually a 'he') would meticulously weigh the various costs and benefits of the potential courses of action (it was also assumed he had perfect information about these relative costs and benefits of each) to arrive at the perfect decision to maximise his total 'utility'—a fancy word for happiness or wellbeing.

According to this 'theory of consumer choice', perfectly rational consumers faced with a 'budget constraint' (basically, the amount of money available to spend) choose between competing 'consumption bundles'—'Should I buy biscuits or bread?'—and, based on perfect knowledge of their own internal preferences (what makes them happy), repeatedly make optimal decisions about allocating their money.

Ha!

In recent decades, a new field called 'behavioural economics' has drawn insights from psychology and actual human behaviour to look more closely at the way we actually do make decisions.

Turns out, we're all a bit crap at this, really.

As humans, we desire instant gratification, placing a much higher value on the pleasure we might experience today over the even greater pleasure we might enjoy tomorrow from delaying our consumption (a process known as 'hyperbolic discounting'). We also fear potential losses much more than we value potential gains ('loss aversion').

On any given day, we can oscillate between being overconfident or too hesitant, depending on the circumstances. Sometimes we jump the gun; other times we procrastinate. We make different decisions depending on the number of choices we confront ('choice overload') or the particular time of the day ('decision fatigue'). We have trouble juggling our conflicting internal desires (we want to both eat the cake and lose weight).

Sometimes we're not even aware of what our internal preferences are. Always, however, our preferences are shaped heavily by societal expectations, biological drivers, family or peer pressure.

We are exquisitely human—all of us.

That's not to say that we wouldn't all be better off if our decision making did more closely resemble the rational model.

It's just to say that, very often, it doesn't.

Governments bear enormous responsibility to ensure that the financial system we are forced to navigate is a less dangerous place, one in which we are nudged towards making more optimal decisions.

But I also believe we can take the reins a bit more ourselves, if we choose. We can begin to see our decision-making flaws and put in place systems to make us more aware of the explicit choices and trade-offs we face. My budgeting system, for example, helps me to see the trade-off between spending now or saving for the future. It also helps me to overcome my natural 'loss aversion' to investing in the share market. We'll get to that in parts II and III.

For now, just know that you aren't the only one who has struggled a bit with money and that it doesn't always have to be that way.

Debunking money myth #2

OLD THOUGHT	NEW THOUGHT
Some people are just bad at money (and I'm one of them!)	Everyone's a bit crap at money, but with a little knowledge and hard work, anyone can learn to improve their finances.
OLD EMOTIONS	NEW EMOTIONS
Alienated, submissive, inferior	Connected, courageous, hopeful, open
OLD BEHAVIOUR	NEW BEHAVIOUR
I do not attempt to budget, save or invest money.	I make cautious and small steps towards tracking my money.

Money myth #3
Spending money is bad and I'm not supposed to spend

Boy, do I have some good news for you! Some people think being good at money is all about permanent deprivation and eating baked beans your whole life.

But, according to economics, spending money is pretty much the whole point of life!

We are here to spend money on the things we need and want. The point is not just to save but, ultimately, to spend. In fact, pretty much the only point of saving money is that you will, in fact, get to spend it one day.

It's just that you face trade-offs between spending your money today versus spending it in the future.

The irony here is that many of the people who think spending is 'bad' are often the very people who do most of it. As with any natural desire, if you suppress it too hard, it will find a way out.

On the flipside, there are people who worry too much about the future and deny themselves the pleasures available from spending today.

As a generation, I'm actually less worried about my fellow millennials inhaling too many smashed avocados, and more worried they're living in a perpetual state of fear that they're never going to be financially comfortable.

In their textbook *Principles of Economics*, economists Betsey Stevenson and Justin Wolfers (they're married—isn't that cute?) advise us to 'spend more when the marginal value of spending today is more than the marginal benefit of spending a dollar-plus-interest in the future'. (Marginal just means the extra bit of value you get from your new spending).

So, I don't know who needs to hear this today but: it's okay to spend some of your money.

Debunking money myth #3

OLD THOUGHT	NEW THOUGHT
Spending money is bad and I'm not supposed to spend it.	We are here to experience pleasure in life and it's okay to spend some money on things that truly bring me joy!
OLD EMOTIONS	NEW EMOTIONS
Guilty, ashamed, resentful	Joyful, liberated, happy
OLD BEHAVIOUR	NEW BEHAVIOUR
I often end up spending quite a lot of money and feeling terrible about it.	I spend time reflecting on the purchases that I find pleasurable and plan nice activities within my budget.

Money myth #4
There is a perfect way to do money and I'm not doing it

When it comes to arranging your own personal finances, I see so many people obsessed with the 'shoulds'.

Should I rent or buy? Should I invest in shares or property? How should I invest an inheritance? How much should I have in my emergency fund?

We're 'should-ing' ourselves all over the place. I'm going to tackle a few of these thorny issues later in the book, but here's a spoiler alert: there is rarely a one-size-fits-all answer. It's called personal finance for a reason—ultimately, these are personal decisions.

Sure, financial advisors can give advice on which courses of action can minimise your tax or are likely to result in you amassing the greatest wealth. But in reality, they can't predict the future.

And even if they could, only you know if what you have to give up to get those outcomes is worth it to you. Working your whole life in a demanding job to get a fat income in retirement?

Only you know if that trade-off is worth it.

In my experience, however, figuring out what your own internal preferences are can take some time.

I remember in the midst of my divorce a therapist advising me to write a list of things that brought me pleasure and then to do them.

Trouble was, between the push and pull of work, family and friends, I'd lost all sense of what I liked to do—if I ever really knew to begin with.

Since then, however, I've been working on a 'pleasures list'—and I recommend you try writing your own.

Here's mine:

- **coconut-scented hair conditioner**
- **bushwalks**
- **rewatching *The Hobbit* and *The Lord of the Rings***
- **salted pretzel chocolate**
- **hot showers**

- **CrossFit exercise classes**
- **going to bed at 9 pm**
- **orgasms! (You're not supposed to say that out loud, but it's true!)**
- **coffee**
- **sitting on a sun lounge near a pool**
- **scented candles**
- **reading fiction books and attending a book club**
- **journaling**
- **fresh air and staring at blue skies**
- **emails from readers to say I have helped them**
- **weekends away with friends**
- **living in a clean and tidy home that I own.**

Turns out, most of the things on my list are pretty cheap, besides home ownership and CrossFit. But if you want something badly enough, expensive is okay.

Friends, it turns out the entire point of life might just be about figuring out what makes you — as an individual — happy. And doing it.

It helps to know that what you desire might evolve over time. And that's okay.

And when you look back on past decisions, it also helps to know that you did the best you could with the information you had about what you thought would make you happy at the time. And when you know differently, you do differently.

We're not going for perfection here. All we can hope for is better self-observation and deeper self-knowledge.

Debunking money myth #4

OLD THOUGHT	NEW THOUGHT
There is a perfect way to do money and I'm not doing it.	My ideas about what sort of life I want will likely evolve over time, and it's okay to change the plan and learn as I go along.
OLD EMOTIONS	NEW EMOTIONS
Ashamed, inadequate, inferior	Respected, hopeful, confident
OLD BEHAVIOUR	NEW BEHAVIOUR
I avoid making money decisions.	I try new ways of spending, saving and investing money, knowing it might not ever be 'perfect'.

Money myth #5
I've left it too late and I'll never have enough money

This is a really common one.

The reality, however, is that most Australians do retire with enough money to live off, when their private savings are combined with the full or part age pension.

According to a report by the Grattan Institute, many Australians can, in fact, expect to enjoy a higher income in retirement than they had during their working lives, due to the relative generosity of the age pension compared to other working-age welfare payments.

The age pension for singles today is about $25 000 per annum and $38 000 for couples. These numbers will be out of date by the time you read this—and that's a good thing—because the age pension increases every six months in line with wages or inflation, whichever is higher.

The unemployment payment JobSeeker, by contrast, pays just $16 367 and only rises with inflation (which historically rises by less than wages).

So, many Australians will actually get a pay rise in retirement.

So why don't we hear more about this? Why do we keep hearing that the age pension won't exist at some point, or that it'll be too minimal to exist on?

Well, it's worth recognising that the superannuation industry has a vested interest in getting you to save like crazy. They generally get paid a percentage fee on your super balance, after all.

You'll often hear it quoted that you need $45 239 per annum for a 'comfortable' retirement (again, these figures change). That figure is based on a survey by—you guessed it—the superannuation industry itself. It also produces a figure for a 'modest' retirement of $28 775 for singles, which suddenly starts to sound a lot more achievable for many.

Note that none of these figures include rental costs, so the argument for trying to own a home outright in retirement is compelling.

The government is also complicit in the retirement scare campaign. It comes down to a little thing economists call 'moral hazard'. If you knew that the government was going to support you even if you pissed all your money up the wall, mightn't you be a little more inclined to go, well, actually piss it up the wall?

Which is not to say that living on the age pension alone is going to fund a particularly lavish lifestyle, and particularly not if you don't own a home.

But it's something. And it's not going anywhere. When you're old, you also get access to a lot of cool discounts on public transport and medicines.

Of course, the only real way to know what income you might want in retirement is to track and project your actual spending habits—which we'll get to in parts II and III.

Another really common myth about retirement is that if you're attempting to self-fund, you must save up enough that you can live off the earnings of that money alone. That's not true; you're supposed to start drawing down at least part of the principal of your investments in retirement.

And finally, it's also a myth that the money you accumulate in your family home is inaccessible to fund your retirement. In fact, there are 'reverse mortgage' products and the government's own Pension Loans Scheme, which enable you to spend the equity in your home.

Of course, that eats into the kids' inheritance. But if you need it, or want it, it's there.

Debunking money myth #5

OLD THOUGHT	NEW THOUGHT
I've left it too late and I'll never have enough money.	I can work to build my savings and fortify my future living standards above what the government will give me to keep my head above water.
OLD EMOTIONS	**NEW EMOTIONS**
Frightened, anxious, insecure	Peaceful, hopeful, respected
OLD BEHAVIOUR	**NEW BEHAVIOUR**
I'm either working too hard or scrimping too much in fear of what is to come.	I'm taking small, actionable steps to save for retirement, while also enjoying life today.

Money myth #6
I have to know my 'why' before I can start to improve

Personal finance books often start by insisting you sit down and write out your 'why' behind wanting to be better with money.

For me, it's just too big a philosophical question to begin with. It's essentially asking: what is the meaning of life? There's a reason philosophers have struggled with this question for millennia.

What's my 'why'? I want to be happy, of course! That's all anyone ever wants.

I think what people really need starting out is a system for tracking and mapping their money that is flexible and allows them to continually refine their definition of joy as they grow and learn.

Forget sitting around pondering 'Why?' and start by taking small actions, like tracking your spending and trying to anticipate some of the larger irregular expenses that will lob in the future.

Debunking money myth #6

OLD THOUGHT	NEW THOUGHT
I have to know my 'why' before I can start.	When it comes to money, it's best to start with small, actionable steps and build up to the bigger questions.
OLD EMOTION	**NEW EMOTION**
Perplexed, confused, overwhelmed	Optimistic, open, inquisitive

OLD BEHAVIOUR	NEW BEHAVIOUR
I'm procrastinating and not doing anything to improve my finances.	I'll start tracking my spending and investigating where my money is going.

Which brings me to my final thought …

Money myth #7
Budgeting is boring

This one makes me smile. It reminds me of when children protest about even the smallest tasks, like putting on their shoes or brushing their teeth.

You see, saying you think budgeting is boring and you don't want to track your spending is a bit like having an adult tantrum about not wanting to put on your shoes.

Grow up, sugar. Welcome to life.

Could it be that, at heart, you're not really bored by budgeting, but that you're just upset that money doesn't grow on trees and you can't have everything you want?

Well, you can't have everything you want, but you can have *some* of it. And you can have it guilt- and worry-free if you learn to budget. And what could be more interesting than getting the things you want?

Debunking money myth #7

OLD THOUGHT	NEW THOUGHT
Budgeting is boring.	I'm an adult now and I get to choose how I spend my money—isn't that cool?
OLD EMOTIONS	**NEW EMOTIONS**
Apathetic, indifferent, bored	Playful, interested, joyful
OLD BEHAVIOUR	**NEW BEHAVIOUR**
I have no idea where my money is going.	I'll read the rest of this book and learn the 'Money with Jess' method for tracking and managing money (go you!).

●●●

Now, at this point I can practically hear you screaming, 'Jess, thank you for liberating me of my destructive thoughts about money!'

'I am ready to forge ahead and translate these new, healthier thoughts into tangible and manageable steps to start taking control of my money and building wealth!'

To which I say, first of all: that's great! That was the entire point of this chapter! I'm so glad it worked.

And also: hold your horses.

Before I start teaching you the system I use for managing my own money, there's someone I want you to meet …

3

It's time to meet Future You...

I think a big part of the problem we face when thinking about money is that it involves both making assumptions about an uncertain future and, to some degree, confronting our own mortality: the fact that we are all going to age, and eventually die.

Bummer, right? And kind of scary, too. I get it; I feel that pinch of fear too.

We also live in a culture that idolises youth and often fails to reserve enough admiration and love for our elders. Aging then, is something to avoid — or to avoid thinking about, at least.

As I mentioned earlier, humans also have a tendency to engage in 'hyperbolic discounting', which is devaluing the future pleasure we can expect to get from delaying spending money today.

So a lot of the mental work behind getting good at managing money and smoothing our spending out over our entire lifespans (remember, that's the big, hairy goal for all of us) lies in confronting our fears about growing old.

It helps if we can find some way to connect emotionally to our future self: to see that person as real and begin to prioritise their needs and desires, too. If we feel affection for our future self, it is more likely we will want to take good care of them.

So let's just stop for a hot minute and face our fears together, shall we? It's time to introduce yourself to Future You.

A great way to do this is to use one of those 'face tune' apps you can get on your smartphone. Remember that craze? Essentially, you take a selfie, upload it to the app and it automatically alters your features in some way. You can give yourself purple hair or change your gender, or — importantly — predict what you will look like when you're older.

Here's me, I'm guessing when I'm about 60 or 70 …

You mightn't notice much of a difference, but I do. I think it's easier to see differences when you're looking at your own face. I can see the changes: a few more wrinkles, a more jowly neck.

A word of warning: some of these apps can make Future You look like a hideous zombie, so be careful which one you use. And do your future self a favour by applying a few nice filters, if necessary.

Have some fun, but most importantly, try to really sit with your image and imagine that this is you in a few decades' time. Because it will be. If you're fortunate enough to get to that age, that is.

While we're at it, and just for a laugh, check out this hunk …

(Is it okay to be a bit attracted to yourself as the opposite sex? Asking for a friend …)

Moving on.

Another really great way to come to grips with Future You is to write a letter to them expressing your hopes for them.

The trick is to visualise them as someone you really care for and want to see thrive (if you can manage to get that visual of me as a man out of your head, that is — I certainly can't).

Okay, I'll go first …

Dear Future Jess,

Girl! You are rockin' that bob cut!

Anyway, what I really want to know is this: are you happy? Did I look after you well enough? Do you have enough money? Are you in good health? Are you accepting the changes in your body with good grace? Do you finally love your body for what it can do, rather than what it looks like? You know how I always struggled with that. Did you ever manage to deadlift your body weight at the gym?

Are you still working, or did you retire at 60, like I hoped for you at one stage? Do you still live in that lovely little flat I bought for you? I know it wasn't as big as we wanted, but I really didn't want you still to be paying rent at this stage when you're not working. I feel so fortunate I was able to achieve that for us.

So, how much do houses cost now?! Fifty-trillion-something dollars? And those shares we bought in 2021—what are they worth now? Whatever happened to Bitcoin—is that still 'a thing'? Should I have bought some? Any hot stock picks I should know about?

Are we still having pandemics? Did we figure out climate change?

Did you ever resolve that question you grappled with in your early 40s about whether it's necessary to be in a long-term relationship to be happy? Did you fall in love again? With how many people? Did you ever try that thing you always secretly wanted to try …? Of course you did, you saucy minx. 😉

How is our son? Is he happy? Was he really embarrassed by that bit you just wrote in your book? And that bit about orgasms in the last chapter? Oh well. If you're not embarrassing your kids a little bit, are you even living?

I guess if I could wish one thing for you, Future Jess, it's that you feel peaceful and secure. Do you finally have time to read all those books I bought us? Did I invest enough time into nurturing our friendships so that you have nice people to hang out with?

Did you ever hear from any readers about this book? Did it help anyone? Did anyone actually do the letter writing thing? I hope so. I hope it helped them to really focus for a moment on their future selves and visualise some of the things they may want for themselves.

I've gotta admit it, Future Jess, when I first laid eyes on your picture, I recoiled a little. I guess it's only natural to fear getting older: being that much closer to The End. Are you scared about that, too? Or does peace come with age?

Future Jess, how did I do? Did I get the balance right? Did I worry too much? Should I have spent a bit more money now—had a bit more fun?

I hope you're proud of me, Future Jess. I have a sneaking suspicion that you are. I'm doing my best.

Anyway, Future Jess, this book ain't writing itself, so I'd better crack on.

Take care and I'll be you soon. xx

Here are some prompts to help you write your own letter:

- Set aside some quiet time for this. Write your letter by hand or electronically—it doesn't matter. You don't have to do this exercise right now, but I do think it's worth returning to at some stage.

- Picture yourself writing to a Future You at an age when you imagine you'll no longer be working.

- Try to project onto your future self the positive attributes that you wish to have. In my letter, you can see I want Future Jess to be healthy, adventurous and calm.

- What sorts of activities does your Future Self engage in? Ask them about some. What features of your current life do you hope will be the same? Which things would you like to be different?

- Make sure to ask questions about all the things that you deem to be important or valuable in life. Relationships, health and so on. You get to decide which.

- Try to cultivate a sense of intimacy, warmth and connection between the two of you. This should be a relationship of mutual care and admiration. You feel fond towards and admiring of Future You, and Future You is grateful, in return, for all your efforts to get them to where they are. They know you always did the very best you could at the time.

- State any fears you might have for your future self: that you'll be poor, homeless, alone and so on. It can be enough just to acknowledge that you have those fears. Perhaps you could outline some steps you're going to take to minimise the chances of Future You experiencing that as an outcome.

- **Inject some humour—acknowledge and celebrate your mutual quirks!**
- **Imagine for a moment that you may, in fact, get to read your letter again when you actually reach the age you are imagining your future self to be. Your future self is going to be a real person, one day. Now, hold onto that thought.**

I think it's so important to have some notion in your mind of the future self you are looking after when you make decisions about money. Not that their needs should always override yours. But they should at least be considered.

So, the next time you're looking to 'add to cart' that new handbag or aspirational set of ski pants, perhaps you can think twice. Ask yourself: is the pleasure I will get from these today worth more than the pleasure I could deliver to Future Me by saving or investing the money instead?

Only you can know, of course.

But it's important that you at least stop to ask yourself the question.

Okay, before we get to part II of this book, where I begin to introduce you to some of the details of my unique budgeting system and how to use it, I'd like to run you through a pretty simple formula in the next chapter that I developed for making sure you are looking after Future You. It's really the only formula for building wealth you will ever need.

It's also the intellectual framework that underpins my entire budgeting system. So, you know, pretty important to understand.

Then we'll get the highlighters out, okay?

4

The four steps to financial freedom

People have different definitions of what 'financial freedom' means to them.

For some people, it means having so much money they never need to work again.

But for me, financial freedom is not so much a destination—a point in time at which I'll retire—but a state of mind. It's a process I follow to stay on top of my money that gives me that sense of 'financial control' that we know is so important to wellbeing. It's being able to, on a daily basis, make informed decisions about how I spend and invest my money. That's real freedom to me.

My budgeting system gives me that sense of freedom and it's all based around four key steps: generating income, tracking spending, creating a surplus and investing it.

Having a system in place to regularly track and monitor my spending, income and surpluses helps me overcome my inbuilt 'loss aversion' to investing and instead be able to regularly put my money to work.

In this chapter, I break down the four major steps I see as the pathway to achieving this same sense of freedom. It's a basic formula for building wealth that, if repeated consistently over time, will get you to retirement one day.

 ## STEP 1
EARN an income

Do you earn an income? If yes, then congratulations! You are already taking the first step towards financial freedom!

Give yourself a pat on the back.

Of course, not everyone has equal access to life's opportunities, be it because of their family of origin, social class, disabilities or illness. So it is quite common for many households, at times, to need to rely on alternate sources of income, such as social support payments. And that's okay too.

In fact, many such households turn out to be the best budgeters: when money is tightest, we have the greatest incentive to manage it carefully.

Income can also come from a variety of other sources, such as side-hustles, small businesses, child support payments, income protection payouts, workers compensation schemes and income-generating investments such as property or shares.

However you get it, pretty much every household or person will have some sort of income coming in the door.

Step 1 on the path to financial freedom is just to know exactly how much you are earning and to try to maximise this income as much as possible.

I'm always surprised by the number of people who don't know, off the top of their heads, their exact salary. Like, how much do you actually receive into your bank account each year, after your employer has taken out tax and compulsory super contributions?

Can you write a number here: $_____?

If not, it would be well worth putting this book down for a moment to go check your latest payslip and write a number above (come back though, okay?).

Of course, for people in casual work or on variable incomes, this can be hard. In part III, I'll share some advice on how to budget with a variable income.

In terms of how to maximise your income, the best career advice I've come across can basically be distilled into the following phrase: 'Do your weird'. You know, that thing that makes you stand out from the crowd? Do that.

Economists call this pursuing your 'comparative advantage'. It's a theory usually applied at a national level to say countries should specialise in producing the stuff they can produce relatively better than any other country. Sure, you can make widgets. But if another country can make those same widgets more efficiently, you're unlikely to be able to command much pricing power.

So pick a job you can do well that other people can't do as well as you, and you're likely to have success.

Admittedly, this can be bad luck for people for whom the thing they're relatively best at doing is also a job traditionally undervalued by society, like caring for the elderly or children. In this situation, you may have to accept a trade-off between the satisfaction you get from performing your job well and the monetary rewards. And if this is you: thank you for your hard work. It is so important.

Once you know what you're good at, it's time to make sure you're getting paid for the value you produce.

PAY RISE HACKS

My top 9 hacks for getting a pay rise

☐ **Focus on your worth.** Focus any pay negotiations you have on the unique skills and value you bring to your employer. Remember, these skills grow in value over time with experience.

☐ **Market test your value.** Monitor job ads or approach competitor employers. A roving eye is bad in romantic relationships, but entirely appropriate when it comes to your work.

☐ **Ask colleagues what they are paid.** And be willing to share your information too. Most people won't do this because talking about money is taboo. But it could be in your mutual interests to know … and ladies, be sure to ask your male colleagues too.

☐ **Request a 'pay review' with your boss.** If you never ask, you'll never get.

☐ **Prepare a one page summary of all your significant work achievements over the past 12 months.** Be sure to include any ways in which you are acting above your original duties. Take this page into the meeting with you, in case you get nervous. You can also email a copy to your boss when the meeting is over if you forget to mention any relevant points.

- [ ] **Where possible, let your employer make the first offer on the pay rise they are willing to give.** Your employer has more information than you on what salaries they actually pay. So wait and see what they come up with—it just might surprise you (particularly if you're a woman!).

- [ ] **Never accept the first offer.** Full stop. This is a negotiation, remember?

- [ ] **Ask for double the pay rise you want.** So, say you're on a $70000 salary and you really want $80000, ask for $90000. If you ask for double the pay rise you want, you'll be happy when you only get half.

- [ ] **And finally: be prepared to jump ship if the price is right.** If your current employer is unable to match the market rates for your work and you don't highly value other aspects of working for their company, like flexible work, then be prepared to jump ship. If you jump, never volunteer your current salary. Wait for their offer and then ask for more!

STEP 2
TRACK your spending

What many people don't expect about getting pay rises is that they are actually no guarantee of financial freedom. Why not?

It's called 'lifestyle inflation'. You get the higher-paying job so you decide to 'treat yo' self' with a fancier suit, handbag or shoes. Besides, you're shouldering soooo much responsibility now and you're soooo busy, surely you deserve a few nice meals out?

Look at you go! You're killing it climbing the corporate ladder, so it must also be time to live in a more salubrious suburb? Send the kids to private schools? How about a few lavish overseas holidays, as you attempt to squeeze your entire home life into four weeks of annual leave?

Been there. Done that.

Learning to keeping a lid on your expenses, even as your income rises, is key to making progress towards financial freedom.

The key to this, I believe, is to track your spending. You can't know what you don't measure.

So, how much do you spend each year on living expenses? Or each month?

Can you write a number here? $_____

No?

I didn't think so.

Don't worry, not many people can. We will get to this in part II when we perform a complete audit and spring clean of your spending. I hope you're looking forward to that as much as I am!

 ## STEP 3
CREATE a surplus

So, you're earning an income and tracking your spending. Great. Here's a revelation: to have a surplus, you need to spend less than you earn.

If you're not currently doing this, you need to find immediate ways to either increase your income or decrease your spending. In part II, we'll dive into the many ways you can trim your spending—you might be surprised at the savings to be had.

Once you've done this and you are producing a surplus, congratulations: you will have become a 'saver'. You will officially be performing step 3 on the path to financial freedom—perhaps the most important step there is.

My definition of a 'saver' is anyone who, over a given time period, spends less than they earn. You could also say they experience 'positive cash flow'. You can be knee deep in debt and still be a 'saver'. It is never too early or too late to become one.

You can wake up tomorrow, if you like, and decide to be a saver, provided you spend less on that day than you earn (including provisioning for all the irregular costs you incur, like rent and car insurances, which we'll do in parts II and III of this book).

There's an immense satisfaction in knowing you're not living outside your means and not racking up debts. My budgeting system is designed to give you that reassurance, while also giving you the visibility you might need to trim some expenses or boost your income to maximise your surplus.

 ## STEP 4

PROTECT your surpluses

So you're spending less than you earn and creating surpluses. Well done you!

Now it's time to decide what to do you with your surplus funds.

This is the bit that trips people up the most, as there are many potential options to consider. And you have to actually take action to protect your surplus.

For people who have debt, the first step is to decide what amount of your surplus you want to contribute to paying it off faster.

Everyone also needs to set aside some money in a readily accessible 'emergency fund'. Most personal finance experts advocate having three to six months of living expenses set aside (we'll get to estimating your figure for that soon).

Once you have an emergency fund in place and a strategy for paying off your debts, you can look at investing your surplus funds to protect their value over time.

Should you pay off debt or invest first?

I'm often asked whether it's better to pay off your debt entirely before starting to invest. Some personal finance 'gurus' are adamant you must.

I'm of the same mind as that little girl in the taco advertisement: *Porque no los dos?* Why not both?

Of course, you need to take into account your individual preferences. One person might get great personal satisfaction from owning their home outright sooner.

The key question to ask yourself is this: is the annual after-tax return I expect to make from investing this dollar greater or less than the annual interest I will save from shrinking my debt?

All investing involves taking on 'risk'—both the risk that returns will disappoint your expectations and the natural volatility that comes with share or property valuations over time.

Ultimately, you have to decide what the best mix is for you between paying off debt and investing.

I have one exception to the 'you-do-you' rule: do pay off your highest interest-rate debt as a top priority. Credit cards often come with 20 per cent plus interest rates. There aren't many investments in town that give you a guaranteed return like that.

It's so important that you do decide on a strategy for doing something with your surplus. Here's why.

Remember I said money is a medium of exchange? You exchange your time and skills for it and then exchange it to buy the things you need and want.

Another way to look at money is as a 'store of value'. On a day-to-day basis, in most countries today, this is fairly accurate. One dollar hits your bank account today, and tomorrow it buys you roughly the same amount of groceries as it would today.

But over the longer term, money absolutely sucks as a store of value.

That is, money stored as cash does.

Keeping your money in cash is like keeping it in a storage unit with a big gap under the door, through which rats sneak in quietly and gnaw away at your stockpile.

Economists call this process 'inflation', which is basically the idea that the prices we pay for things rise over time. This means a dollar tomorrow buys less than it does today.

Wouldn't it suck if you saved like a demon all your life only for Future You to discover your hard-earned cash has wasted away because you didn't protect it from inflation?

Yes, it would.

So how do we protect our savings from inflation?

Well, the answer to this question has changed dramatically since the start of this century. Prior to that, you could fairly easily stash your money in an online bank account that would grow in line with inflation, plus a little more.

But look what's happened …

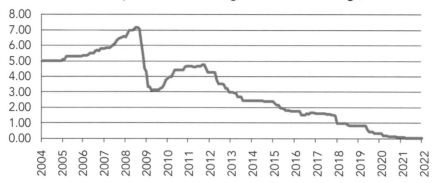

Interest rate paid on online savings accounts containing $10 000

Source: Reserve Bank of Australia 2022

Ouch!

In a world of ultra-low interest rates, protecting your savings requires moving up the 'risk spectrum' and investing your money in assets like property and shares.

Many people find the idea of investing—particularly in shares—completely foreign. Which is why I prefer a mindset of 'protecting'.

Should you invest in property or shares?

First of all, if you're asking this question, it means you're spending less than you earn and have some surplus to invest. Honestly, that's half the battle. Congrats to you! From there, it can often be a matter of personal preference.

I like buying shares because it seems to me that buying tiny pieces of companies gives you a bet on the ability of humans to, over time, find ever smarter and more clever ways to combine the key ingredients of land, labour and capital to produce increasing value over time. It feels like a bet on human evolution—and folks, evolution always wins, in my view. Shares not only tend to appreciate in value over time, but they also pay out 'dividend' income in the meantime—basically a share of the company's profits, which are distributed to shareholders rather than being re-invested in the company. Shares as an asset class, however, are more volatile than property (or perhaps it's just that we get more minute-to-minute information on swings in their value).

On the other hand, I also like property as an investment class, but for more cynical reasons. Over time, governments and societies have shown an inability—or unwillingness, depending how cynical you want to be—to match housing supply to growing housing demand. That pushes up prices over the long term. We may, some day, find a way to fix that. But with about two-thirds of households currently owning property and just one-third renting, the political odds are stacked ever in the favour of rising home values, which makes homeowners feel wealthy and more inclined to vote 'yes' for whichever party delivered them that wealth.

As long as you are investing over a long enough time frame, both shares and property have historically delivered solid returns to investors. Take a look at this:

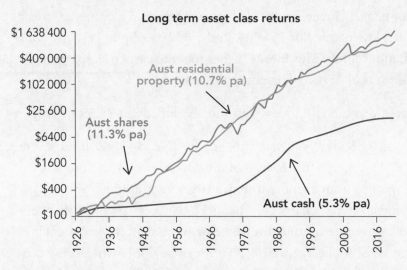

Long term asset class returns

Source: Based on data from ASX, Bloomberg, REIA, AMP

(continued)

You must do your own research on where to invest—I'm not professionally qualified to advise you on that. I do know you should consider the tax implications of any investments you make, your ability to leverage (borrow to buy) your assets, your own risk appetite (which only you can know) and—you guessed it—your own preferences on which asset you enjoy investing in.

Happy investing, folks! It's a nice dilemma to have …

Chances are, you're already an investor through your retirement savings account.

Australians are forced to have 10 per cent (set to rise to 12 per cent by 2025) of their wages transferred directly by their employer into a superannuation account, which is then usually invested in a mix of shares, property and fixed interest assets.

Super is a great way to invest your savings, if you don't mind not seeing your money again until you reach preservation age, which is currently 60 for most people. Super is not taxed at your personal income tax rate, but rather at a low flat rate of 15 cents in the dollar—up to certain annual contributions limits. This means higher income earners, in particular, can save a great deal of tax by investing this way.

Of course, you can also invest your money directly in shares or property.

You can also decide if you want to—or are able to—become a 'leveraged investor'. This means that instead of investing slowly over time, you borrow money from a lender to buy a larger asset upfront. You will, of course, incur interest charges on that debt, but you may hope that your asset will appreciate in value over time by more than those costs. This is common for property investing, but it can be done with shares, too (although banks will typically lend more against property than shares).

You can always talk to a lender or mortgage broker to see how much you may be able to borrow this way and any risks associated with these types of loans.

For now, I just want you to know that there has never been a more important time to adopt an 'investor mindset'. You worked hard to save your money; don't let it be eaten up by inflation.

•••

So there you have it. My four steps to financial freedom: earn, spend, create a surplus and protect it. These are also the key components of my budgeting process to track your income and spending, calculate your resulting surpluses and deploy them.

Of course, once you reach retirement, you get to start drawing down on your accumulated investments. But for those still of working age, this is the magic formula for building your wealth.

I told you money was simple, didn't I?

Here is a pretty chart I created to summarise my four steps to financial freedom.

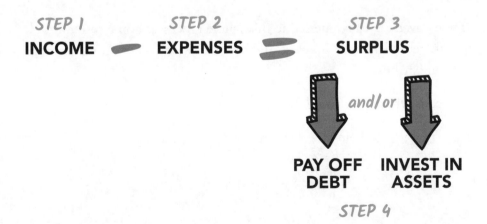

And if this has all gotten a bit heavy for you, here's a picture of a puppy to stare at for a while.

Source: Photo by Hendo Wang on Unsplash

There now, isn't that better?

If you haven't already guessed it, this whole process is going to require you to get much more up close and personal with your existing earning spending habits.

Which is what we're going to begin doing in part II.

I'm so excited to help you start organising your money!

How to create an annual budget

Congratulations! You've managed to read one-third of the way into a book about budgeting! That's no mean feat, my friend. Take a moment to pat yourself on the back and celebrate your achievement.

Also take a moment to appreciate the significant lengths I've gone to thus far to try not to startle you with any trigger words such as 'budget' and 'spreadsheet'.

Eew, amirite? *shudders*

I believe the reason many people recoil when they see or hear the word 'budget' is because it signals something overly restrictive, akin to a diet. That word—'diet'—also gets a bad rap. This is because it's usually associated with a particular *kind* of diet—that is, one where the amount of food consumed is restricted to less than a person's daily calorie requirement, with the goal of achieving weight loss.

In nutrition studies, however, the word 'diet' is just used to describe the total food consumed by a person or society. It doesn't specify whether that consumption leads to weight loss or not. Take, for example, the Mediterranean diet. This term arose from a 1960s observational study of the food consumed by people living in Greece, Italy and Spain. It was only later that it came to mean something quite different, namely a rigid set of rules to follow to achieve weight loss.

The same sort of confusion happens with the word 'budget'. A lot of people seem to instinctively believe a budget is something that will result in deprivation that will force them to eat baked beans and stare at a wall for entertainment.

Again, this is a perversion of the original word. As we learned in chapter 2, it's just a 'thought' about the meaning of the word 'budget'. It's not a fact.

In fact, a 'budget' is simply a statement of what you earn and spend over a certain time period, along with some calculation of the resulting surplus or deficit.

A budget can be as simple as a piece of paper on which you write your estimated income, expenses, and resulting surplus or shortfall. Yes, this information will show you if you're saving money or not. But the budget itself is agnostic as to whether you *should* be saving, or by how much. That's entirely up to you.

The real purpose of a budget is to give you a picture of your overall financial situation. You might be scared about what that picture could ultimately reveal, but a budget can't hurt you. In fact, I believe it can only help by giving you the clarity you need to start making better decisions about where to allocate your precious money.

Governments regularly produce annual budgets that tally their anticipated spending—including welfare, healthcare and the military—against anticipated revenue—including taxes on workers' wages and company profits. Sometimes the result is an annual surplus (revenue exceeds spending) and sometimes it's a deficit (spending exceeds revenue).

These budgets are highly anticipated news events and reporting on them is usually the highlight of my working year! It's important to remember these budgets are always just 'estimates'—a treasurer's best guess of what is to come.

While they get significantly less attention for doing so, throughout the year the Department of Finance also releases monthly budget statements to show actual spending and revenue outcomes. Then, at the end of the financial year, a final budget outcome is declared.

Well, I reckon if it's good enough for the government, it's good enough for you and me!

The purpose of part II of this book is to teach you how to become the treasurer of your own life by creating your very own annual budget. (Later, in Part III, I'll also teach you how to track your actual monthly budget outcomes, just like the Department of Finance does. Over time, tracking your actual outcomes will help you to hone and improve your annual budget estimates. But for now, it's totally fine to just have a guess.)

First, in chapter 5, I'll convince you why having a budget is such a good idea. I'll also share the journey I went on to design, whittle and perfect my unique 10-category budgeting system.

Then, in chapter 6, I'll help you to identify every possible expense you might need to include in your budget. This is where I see budgets often come a cropper because people fail to anticipate a big expense, get downhearted and quit. Trust me: my 10 budget categories are very comprehensive! I've also provided more than 300 money-saving hacks to help you trim your expenses and boost your income. You're so welcome! 😊

Finally, in chapter 7 I'll help you draw all this information together to create your very own annual budget identifying your total income, spending and resulting annual surplus or deficit.

As we go through, I'll be asking you to fill out estimates of all your expenses and, later, your income.

This might all sound completely nerdy to you, but it's no mere academic exercise. I firmly believe that creating a budget is the foundation stone upon which all good money decisions are built.

Let the budgeting begin!

5

Why you need a budget

Take it from me, as you progress through life, you will encounter a surprising number of scenarios in which people in positions of authority expect you to be entirely across the intimate details of your financial life.

If you want to buy a home, retire comfortably or borrow to build wealth, you're going to need an idea of your annual spending.

This was brought home to me when, after a couple of years of searching for my dream first home, I finally decided to get serious about applying for a home loan. I vividly remember the day.

The sun was belting down as I spent several hours pounding the pavement of my local high street, walking in and out of three big-name banks. The staff I encountered in each were friendly and welcoming enough, until things invariably took a turn for the worse when they began bamboozling me with a series of questions to which I did not know the answer.

How much do you spend on food each month? How about trips to the doctor? How much is your health insurance? How much do you spend on petrol?

The questions were all, of course, designed to test how much spare capacity I'd have, after paying for my regular living expenses, to service the repayments on a loan.

In reality, I had no clue, although I did my best to give them a guesstimate.

Knowing your numbers is also crucial when it comes to planning for your retirement. Trust me, at around the age of 40 you'll begin to take a sudden and intense interest in this. To know if you can retire comfortably, you're supposed to also know how much income you'll need each year to cover your living expenses. If you don't know this number, retirement calculators will default to some national average that will, unfortunately, be wildly inaccurate for most people.

Yes, I know retirement may sound *really* far away to some of you. Then again, some younger people I know are really keen on the idea of FIRE: 'Financial Independence, Retire Early'. In order to embrace FIRE, you also need some idea of your anticipated future living expenses.

In the meantime, knowing your annual living expenses will also help you to figure out how big an emergency fund you should have. An emergency fund is a pot of easily accessible money you set aside to crack open in the event of a life emergency, such as if your car gives up the ghost, you incur an unexpected medical bill or you lose your job.

Most personal-finance experts will advise you to have an emergency fund that covers three or six months of your total living expenses. They will also assume you know what that number is. Chances are, you don't.

So how much do you spend each month, or each year? How much does it cost to keep you and your household fed, clothed, sheltered, transported, entertained and everything else you could possibly need or want?

Go on, take a wild guess …

Perhaps you have some idea.

Or perhaps, if you're anything like I was, you have no clue. In which case, fear not! I'm about to share with you a process for figuring it out that I went to significant lengths to design earlier …

My quest to design the ultimate household budgeting system

My home loan application process had a happy ending. Turns out I was comfortably able to borrow enough to buy my first home, which I did.

But as I strapped myself into my massive mortgage, I decided I wanted to know *for sure* that I was indeed capable of comfortably servicing it.

For the first time in my life, I set about creating a realistic annual budget to allay my concerns.

The first thing I did was punch the estimates I had provided to my bank into an Excel spreadsheet (eew, there's that word again). Even for a numbers nerd like me, this was an intimidating process initially.

To keep things fun, I titled the document *Jess' amazingly fun and fantastic and not at all boring or scary budget spreadsheet.*

I then set about listing all my income and expenses to see if I really did have enough to keep myself in the black.

For most people, identifying their income sources is a relatively simple affair. It's the spending side of a budget that usually catches people out because there are so many possible expenses to account for. How to sort them all logically?

I began to ask myself, had I really considered every potential expense in the estimate of living expenses I had given to the bank? Had I remembered, for example, to provide for new tyres every couple of years? Or a new car battery? What about emergency repairs if my fridge or washing machine broke down? Or little things such as batteries, makeup and home décor?

I became hell bent on making sure I had accounted for every possible expense that could come up in my life.

My first stop was to consult with some of the highest order numbers nerds in the land at the Australian Bureau of Statistics (ABS).

I knew from my work as a finance journalist that this group of awesome boffins conducts a regular survey to capture every facet of Australian household spending (known as the Household Expenditure Survey).

Every couple of years the boffins recruit a brave band of Aussies willing to keep a meticulous spending diary for a week recounting every single good or service they purchase during that time. These selfless souls are then subjected to further questioning about any infrequent purchases—such as cars and fridges—that fall outside the survey week.

The most recent survey was conducted in 2015–16 and the boffins were able to code out about 700 individual goods and services Aussies spend their money on: from dental floss, to video games, to gas cylinders for the barbecue.

Here are their topline results.

Average annual household expenditure on goods and services

Current housing costs	$ 14 508
Domestic fuel and power	$ 2132
Food and non-alcoholic beverages	$ 12 324
Alcoholic beverages	$ 1664
Tobacco products	$ 676
Clothing and footwear	$ 2288
Household furnishings and equipment	$ 3016
Household services and operation	$ 2340
Medical care and health expenses	$ 4264
Transport	$ 10 762
Communication	$ 2444
Recreation	$ 8944
Education	$ 2288
Personal care	$ 1508
Miscellaneous goods and services	$ 5044
Total goods and services expenditure	**$ 74 200**

Source: © Australian Bureau of Statistics.
Note: figures may not add up due to rounding.

Not to disrespect the boffins, but I found their categorisation system a little clunky, and far too cluttered.

So I decided to tidy it up!

I am a longtime and ardent fan of the diminutive Japanese tidying guru Marie Kondo and her prescription for sorting all your household belongings according to category, starting with clothes, then books, and so on.

When tidying up my room as a child, I used to pack things away according to their colour. I'd start by putting away everything white, followed by yellow items, then orange … you get the picture.

So, as I set about designing my budgeting system, I decided to combine the Kondo method with my own colour-coding method by first dividing all possible human spending into categories and then giving each a different splash of colour!

I downloaded the Bureau of Statistics' spreadsheet of 700 or so individual spending items and began dividing them up into a neat set of just 10 spending categories, each of which I lovingly named. I designed the category names to reflect the fundamental need or want the spending was attempting to fulfil.

My 10 spending categories are:

1. Housing
2. Household
3. Utilities
4. Transport
5. Food
6. Health
7. Education
8. Appearance
9. Lifestyle
10. Professional fees.

With a satisfaction level akin to placing the last piece into a giant jigsaw puzzle, I was able to find a home for every one of the expenses within my 10 spending categories.

Aaaaaahhhhh.

Keen to confirm my results and to check if I'd missed anything, I reviewed the results of similar household expenditure surveys in the United States, the UK, Canada and New Zealand. Turns out, there are surprising commonalities.

Finally, I trawled through a 265-page document produced by the United Nations in 2018 titled *Classification of Individual Consumption According to Purpose* to make sure I hadn't missed anything.

I hadn't.

Basically, it seems there are only so many things human beings can spend money on!

I can't tell you how much joy it brought me to realise I could confidently sort every single item of household spending into my 10 neat categories. And just when I thought I couldn't have any more fun, I came across the idea of assigning a different coloured highlighter to each of my expense categories. (I track my spending by hand, so having a colour for each category helps me to easily sort my spending. More on this in part III.)

Finally, with a feeling I can only describe as approaching ecstasy, I bought myself a labelling machine so I could print a label for each highlighter, to display its assigned category name. Different (highlighter) strokes for different folks, okay?

Here's a picture of my beauties. I couldn't be more proud of them.

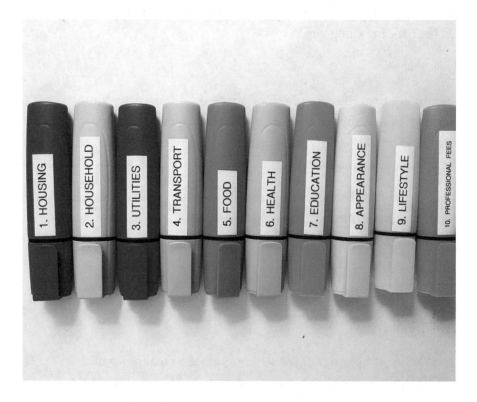

In the next chapter, I'll run you through each of my categories in turn along with all the expenses you need to consider for each to compile your own annual budget. You will have space on the pages of this book to tally your costs by hand, or you can download a PDF or Excel version of my Annual Budget worksheet from my website, jessicairvine.com.au. Or you can simply punch your estimates into a document on your device, or scribble them in a blank notebook. Whatever works best for you!.

I'm so excited for you to begin reading chapter 6; it's honestly my favourite chapter in the book.

I passionately believe the reason most people's attempts at budgeting fail is because while creating a budget is the first thing most personal finance and budgeting experts advise, they also usually leave it up to you to figure out your own categories for expenses. This runs the significant risk of you forgetting to plan for a lot of the less frequent but often quite large expenses in your life.

You think you're doing well and then suddenly—*boom!* Your car registration bill falls due, torpedoing all your carefully laid plans, and you give up.

Friends, I don't like surprises. And I doubt you do either.

But there's no need to worry because I've done all the hard work of identifying every possible expense you could face in your lifetime. All you have to do is work methodically through the 10 budget categories in chapter 6 and identify the expenses that currently apply to your household.

Then, in chapter 7, we'll tally up your estimates of your total household expenses against your estimated annual income and voilà! You'll have created an annual budget!

Now doesn't that sound like fun? Not at all boring or scary. ☺

6

My 10 budget categories explained

We're about to step through each of my 10 budget categories in turn. The purpose of this chapter is to run you through every possible expense you might need to consider when assembling your own budget. Then, in chapter 7, we'll tally it all up for a complete snapshot of your household income and expenditure.

But first, here are some instructions on how to make the most of this chapter.

- To begin, I'd like you to have a pen—or pencil—and a set of 10 different-coloured highlighters handy. Choose one highlighter to represent each category.

- For each category, I'll be asking you to enter (right here in this book—unless you're doing this on a screen) an estimate of what you believe you spend on that expense category each year.

- As you finish entering each estimate, highlight it using the highlighter colour you chose for that category. Some people don't like writing in books, but I give you permission!

- Alternatively, you can download my Annual Budget worksheet in PDF or spreadsheet form from my website, jessicairvine.com.au and enter your figures there. I do believe there are benefits to recording things manually (which I'll explain in part III of this book) but you do what suits you best.

- For each spending sub-category, I've provided space for you to write a weekly, fortnightly, monthly, quarterly or annual figure. Simply write or type in a figure for the frequency you actually pay, or whichever frequency makes most sense to you. For example, if you pay your council rates quarterly, record your latest bill amount in the quarterly space. Then tally up an annual estimate for each sub-category (we'll use these figures in chapter 7 to compile a snapshot of your total annual expenses). For example, if you entered $400 quarterly for electricity, you would multiply this by 4 and write $1600 in the 'annually' space. If you only want to make an annual estimate for a sub-category, that's fine — just write a number under 'Annually' and nothing in the other columns.

- Take your time. Use bank statements, bills, receipts or anything else you can lay your hands on that will give you this information — or just give it your best guess. Part of the work is in realising you don't know, and that perhaps you need to track your spending to find out (which I'll help you do in chapter 8).

- For sub-categories that don't apply to you at all — for example, if you don't own a car, so you don't need to pay car maintenance — enter '$0'. Depending on your life stage, some items won't apply to you now, but may in the future. You can always revisit this chapter as your life evolves, you have kids, you buy a home, and so on. Budgets evolve, and that's ok.

- Remember that monthly figures are annual figures divided by 12, not weekly figures multiplied by 4 (you'd be surprised how many people get caught out by that!). And that there are 26 fortnights in a year.

- As you start to lay out all your spending, you will invariably find areas where you would like to trim back. To that end, I have jam-packed this chapter full of money-saving hacks. Use a pen to tick any hacks you'd like to try. Alternatively, you can ignore these hacks for now and revisit them when you've finished completing your annual budget if you'd like to explore ways to save.

- Take breaks as needed. I doubt you'll be able to do this all in one sitting. Work methodically through each category, filling in estimates as you go. If you're unsure, just put down something—anything will do for now. You can always refine and revisit this over time as you get a better idea of your actual spending.

Okay, I think that's it! Here we go …

HOUSING
Put a roof over your head

It should come as no surprise that housing—the need to put a roof over your head—takes pride of place as the first of my budget categories.

Shelter is one of the most fundamental of human needs and by far the single biggest expense for most households of working age.

It's also the easiest category to fill out as there's only one number you need to know.

If you're a renter, the number is your rent: what you pay to a landlord, boarding house, parent or anyone else to live in their property.

If you have a mortgage, the number to write down is your minimum required mortgage repayment. If you make additional payments, don't include them here. We're trying to come up with an estimate of what it costs you to live. Paying extra off the mortgage is actually a form of saving—something you do with your surplus funds after you've deducted your expenses from your income—so it's not an expense.

Go ahead and write a figure for either your rent or mortgage payments in the appropriate column on the next page (for example, if you make a monthly mortgage repayment, your figure will go under 'Monthly').

	Weekly	Fortnightly	Monthly	Quarterly	Annually
Housing					

Then, also calculate an annual figure for your housing cost and record it under the 'Annually' column. This will help speed things up later on in chapter 7 when we compile your annual budget. And go on, why not highlight your figure with the highlighter colour you've selected for 'Housing'. Feels so good. Trust me.

Congratulations! You've taken the first step to creating your annual budget! Not so hard after all, right?

A note for owners of multiple properties

Only include here the cost of home loans on your principal place of residence — where you live most of the time — plus any other residences you also pay for but do not lease out, such as holiday homes.

After much conferment with the nerds at the Bureau of Statistics, I've determined that expenses incurred on investment properties need to be accounted for separately under 'Income'. Rather than including those costs in your primary household budget as expenses, keep a separate account of your net investment returns from those properties (rent minus costs). If your net returns are positive, include them as a positive source of income in your household budget. If they are negative, also record them under income, but as a negative, reducing your overall income. Also remember that it's the 'after tax' income that matters, so reduce your figures by any tax you expect to pay.

By the way, if you have a holiday home, can I come visit?

Deciding whether to rent or buy

The question of whether to rent or buy a property is a hot button topic, particularly for younger Australians increasingly priced out of home ownership by escalating prices. A new generation is wondering if they can 'rent-vest' by continuing to rent and invest their savings in investment properties or shares.

Here's my take on this question.

Should you rent or buy?

As with most 'should' questions, the answer here is a combination of 'It depends', 'I can't say for sure' and 'What would you prefer?'

If you rent, you're essentially paying for the service of a landlord giving you a place to live in.

Buying a home with a home loan, on the other hand, is a funny mix of paying for a service (the interest you pay to the bank to lend you money) and investment. Why is it a form of investment? Well, when you make repayments on the principal of your loan, you're actually increasing your ownership stake in an investment, namely your property. There is no equivalent for renting, unless you specifically invest some of your savings. With a mortgage, it's forced on you.

So when you're comparing the cost of renting versus buying, it's important to compare the cost of renting against the interest costs you will face borrowing to buy—not the total repayments you will have to make. Rent money and interest money are both 'dead money'!

(continued)

You need to run the numbers on which service (rent payments or interest payments) you think will prove more costly in the long run.

As property values have skyrocketed around the world compared to incomes, this decision has, of course, become a particularly fraught and often emotional one for younger generations.

Some people enjoy the freedom of permanently renting. Life-long renters avoid some of the bigger hidden costs of home ownership, such as property transaction taxes and maintenance.

It's important for rent-vestors to realise, however, that they will face ongoing costs in retirement that homeowners won't (assuming homeowners manage to pay their mortgage off before then). Homeowners also get access to incredible tax benefits, including, in Australia, the complete exemption of capital gains on principal residences from tax. The family home is also excluded from the assets test for the age pension.

In addition, home ownership carries the major benefit that banks are often more willing to lend larger sums earlier in life to people to buy a home than to people who want to rent and invest in shares. And the earlier you get ownership of a large asset, the longer the period over which you get to enjoy any resulting gains.

However, provided you have a laser-like focus on savings, combined with a strategy to leverage, rent-vesting can be an option for people who do not value the non-monetary benefits of home ownership, such as security of tenure and wanting to bang nails in walls.

If you're more attracted to home ownership, please keep reading and I'll share my best hacks for helping you get there.

But first, for the renters, here are some ways of saving.

HOUSING HACKS

My top 9 savings hacks for renters

I can't lie, whether you can score much of a discount on your rent will depend a lot on the local rental market you're in and the relative balance between supply of available properties and demand by potential tenants. But here are some ideas.

- [ ] **Check rental listings in your area.** Stay aware of what similar properties are going for in your area. This will put you in a stronger position to either ask (politely!) for a rental reduction or to push back against proposed increases.

- [ ] **Ask your neighbours what they are paying in rent.**

- [ ] **Look up data on recent trends in rental prices in your area**—rents do not always rise!

- [ ] **Consider asking for a discount on an existing rental** or making a lower offer on an advertised property if you have a good income and a solid rental history. You can only ask!

- [ ] **If you receive a rental increase notice, contact your agent or landlord to request a smaller increase**, or for a delay to the introduction of the increase. Present evidence of comparable rents in your area. You could also offer to sign a longer lease—some landlords are attracted to the stability of retaining good tenants.

- [ ] **Know your tenancy rights.** Tenants unions and advocacy groups can be a great source of information and support.

- [ ] **If the rent increase is too much and you can find a cheaper place, consider moving.** There are costs involved, but the savings may be worth it.

(continued)

□ **Consider renting as part of a share house or renting out any spare rooms**—just don't fall foul of any provisions in your rental agreement against sub-letting.

□ **Live with your mum and dad for a bit longer.** I hate to say it, and it only really applies to people who intend to buy soon, but could you?

How to own your dream home sooner

The day I plastered a 'PURCHASED' sticker on the billboard outside my home remains one of the proudest days of my life. Every day since, I have been extremely grateful for the security and peace of mind home ownership has brought me. It is so nice to be able to check out of the FOMO (fear of missing out) that first home buyers suffer when prices skyrocket.

I also know that I can expect to be rent-free in retirement, meaning that if everything else goes wrong, I can live out a modest life on the age pension (with my home being excluded from the age pension assets test), supplemented by the Pension Loans Scheme to unlock some equity as income, if needed. That's not likely to happen. But it's nice to know the worst-case scenario for me.

Buying my home was the culmination of an arduous and dizzyingly complex process of applying for finance and searching for a property. I wish I had known earlier what I know now about how to deal with lenders to maximise your borrowing capacity. Here is what I reckon is the secret sauce.

How to maximise your borrowing capacity

What ultimately determines your capacity to borrow is how much extra cash flow you have after you deduct your living expenses from your income.

But get this. According to a recent federal court decision in Australia, it is not your 'actual' living expenses that matter, but what a lender might reasonably deem is sufficient for a household like yours. As the judge concluded in the now infamous case: 'I may eat Wagyu beef every day washed down with the finest Shiraz but, if I really want my new home, I can make do on much more modest fare'. Get that? The banks are no longer strictly required to assess you on your current *actual* living expenses, but can apply an estimate of a 'modest' lifestyle for a borrower like you.

In practice, banks commonly apply a figure for your living expenses known as the Household Expenditure Measure (HEM). It is a series produced by the Melbourne Institute, based on the Bureau of Statistics spending data that I used to do my budget categories. The HEM is described by its authors as a 'measure that reflects a modest level of household expenditure for various types of Australian families, excluding expenditure on housing'. The HEM excludes some costs—such as strata/body corporate fees, private school fees, life insurance, student debt payments, child support payments and overseas holidays—which the bank should ask you about separately.

The HEM data itself is not publicly available, but bank loan assessors and mortgage brokers know what it is. Just ask them politely to tell you. You may find it is a lot lower than your actual expenditure, in which case, learning how to trim your expenses to something resembling it will probably help you boost your borrowing power and secure the home you want.

(continued)

Using some mortgage broker data I obtained on the minimum living expenses figures used in the serviceability calculators of 19 different lenders, I pulled out the most commonly used figures— used by nine of the lenders—in the following table. I checked with the Melbourne Institute and they said these figures looked in the ballpark of the HEM (at the time of writing), while not being the actual HEM figures (which are adjusted for inflation regularly).

The table shows the living expense figures for a single adult with no children, living in inner-city Sydney.

Living expense figures for a single adult with no children, living in inner-city Sydney

Person's annual income	Monthly living expense	Annual living expense
$40 000	$1217	$14 604
$60 000	$1453	$17 436
$80 000	$1681	$20 172
$100 000	$1985	$23 820
$120 000	$2260	$27 120
$140 000	$2618	$31 416
$160 000	$2776	$33 312
$180 000	$2967	$35 604

This is just a ballpark guide as to what banks might consider a reasonable estimate of your living expenses. Of course, actual living expenses will vary between households depending on each household's unique circumstances. And the banks will ask you to provide additional figures about your 'non-HEM' spending on things such as private school fees and child support payments, which are not included in the figures above.

The whole point of part II of this book is to tally up your current *actual* living expenses. At the end, you'll be able to see how your living expenses compare with the table above. Chances are, they'll be higher, depending on how modestly you're living. So, finding ways to really trim your costs and learning to live to a more modest living standard will definitely turbocharge your borrowing power.

The bottom line is you don't have to give lenders a 'Shiraz and Wagyu' estimate of your spending: a 'tap water and beef mince' estimate will do just fine. Just make sure you can actually live up to it when you get your loan, and always borrow responsibly.

Of course, there are many other things to consider when attempting to buy your first home. Here are my 10 top hacks to get you those keys sooner.

HOUSING HACKS
My 10 top hacks for buying your first home

☐ **Adjust your expectations.** Acknowledge that homes are worth what people are willing and able to pay for them, not what you think they're worth. This can be hard, I know.

☐ **Approach lenders or brokers early on to find out what your maximum borrowing capacity is.** I spent a good deal of time insisting I should only borrow a certain amount before I gave up and began begging lenders to see how much they would lend me.

☐ **Ask lenders what living expenses they would expect to see** for a household of your size, income and location.

(continued)

☐ **Know that you don't need a 20 per cent deposit to buy a home**, even though this might be the ideal and certainly was for previous generations. It is possible to get a foothold in the property market with a much smaller deposit. Again, ask a lender or broker what may be possible. Lenders will commonly charge lenders mortgage insurance (LMI) on mortgages with deposits of less than 20 per cent, but this cost can be amortised into the total cost of the loan.

☐ **Investigate the Australian Government's First Home Loan Deposit Scheme**, under which you can get a loan with just 5 per cent deposit and pay no LMI (eligibility criteria apply). Single parents can also access a scheme to help them buy (LMI free) with just a 2 per cent deposit.

☐ **Research the government's First Home Super Saver Scheme**, if you're not planning to buy for a couple of years. It enables you to save in the low-tax environment of super.

☐ **Access the bank of Mum and Dad**, if you're lucky enough that you can. Parents can either give you cash towards your deposit or go 'guarantor' on your loan to avoid LMI.

☐ **Always at least take a look at some potential homes a suburb or two outside the area you have your heart set on.**

☐ **Consider apartment or townhouse living.** Ground floor apartments can feel surprisingly home-like. Just be aware that you will likely pay strata fees on multi-occupancy homes.

☐ **Pick a place that you could see yourself living in for a decade or so**—otherwise, if you move too often, you'll incur big costs in transaction taxes (such as stamp duty), which apply each time you buy a new home in Australia. One of the best ways to save money is to avoid paying taxes!

How to get the best deal on your mortgage

Many people are so relieved to finally be in their dream home that they just let their home loan become 'set and forget'.

That can be a very costly mistake because lenders apply what is known colloquially as a 'loyalty tax'. That's to say they generally offer their most attractive interest rates and offers to new customers in an attempt to grow their business.

Once they have you on the hook, they no longer have an incentive to ensure you're getting the best rate. So it's up to you to either keep being a new customer — by switching lenders — or threatening to become one by telling your current lender you will leave if they don't give you a better deal.

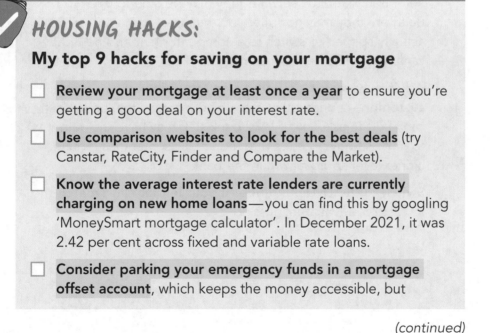

HOUSING HACKS:

My top 9 hacks for saving on your mortgage

- [ ] **Review your mortgage at least once a year** to ensure you're getting a good deal on your interest rate.

- [ ] **Use comparison websites to look for the best deals** (try Canstar, RateCity, Finder and Compare the Market).

- [ ] **Know the average interest rate lenders are currently charging on new home loans** — you can find this by googling 'MoneySmart mortgage calculator'. In December 2021, it was 2.42 per cent across fixed and variable rate loans.

- [ ] **Consider parking your emergency funds in a mortgage offset account**, which keeps the money accessible, but

(continued)

reduces the value of your loan by whatever amount is sitting there — which in turn reduces the interest you pay.

☐ **Consider fixing a portion of your loan for a period of time if fixed interest rates are lower than variable rates.** This is not always the case, and be aware, though, that there can be early repayment costs for breaking the fixed term. Fixed interest loans generally don't allow extra repayments — or only for a limited amount. And they don't generally allow offset accounts. Consider a bet each way with a 'split' loan — split between a fixed interest rate portion and a variable interest rate portion.

☐ **Ring your bank to ask for a lower interest rate and be prepared to play ball.** Say you are looking to refinance and you have found a better deal (ideally you have found one on a comparison website). If you get no joy, ask to speak to their 'retention team' to see what they may be able to offer you. Be aware they may not offer you their best deal until you have actually applied to switch to a competitor lender. And if they can't match a lower interest rate ...

☐ **Ask if they can do anything else to retain you as a loyal customer** — a once-off waiver on your annual fee, perhaps. It can't hurt to ask. Lower level bank staff may have the authority to do this, while interest rate reductions sometimes require higher level approval within the bank.

☐ **Switch to the cheaper lender if your lender can't match the lowest rate available.** Just do it.

□ **Look out for 'cash back' offers for switching to a new lender.** They may pay as much as $4000 to lure you to switch, which should more than cover the costs of discharging your loan with your old lender. Best of all, cash-back offers are tax-free, as the tax office considers them part of your loan refinance, not income. Just make sure the total interest savings on your new loan are worth it.

Okay, did you enter a number in the housing costs table? Did you highlight it with the colour you've chosen for this category?

Great, let's move on.

HOUSEHOLD
Make your house a home

Now that we've put a roof over your head, it's time to make it a home!

I think Darryl Kerrigan, a character in the 1990s cult Australian movie *The Castle*, said it best: 'A man's home is his castle'. The urge to nest and make one's home a pleasant space is deeply rooted in the human psyche.

Which is why my second budget category, Household, is one of my favourites. It also contains a long list of sub-categories containing expenses people often forget to consider when establishing their budget.

Here we remember to cover off on all the costs of repairing and maintaining both your home and garden, along with the costs of decorating and furnishing it and keeping it stocked with all your essentials supplies, such as cleaning and basic hygiene products. Yep, your toilet paper goes here!

We will also look at some of the bigger and less frequent costs of running a household, including home and contents insurance policies and, for home owners, local council fees (yay for renters, for whom these are usually covered in the rent you pay).

For apartment or unit owners, we include here your strata or body corporate fees, cover things like the costs of building maintenance, gardening and insurance, depending on your building.

Maintaining a home is not cheap and things inevitably break. In the estimates that follow, be sure to include an annual sum to cover the repair or replacement of major household appliances and furniture. I usually set aside about $500 a year for this.

Let's get nesting!

Furniture

Understandably, the first thing most people do when they move into a new home is to go out and buy lots of new expensive furniture. Please don't do this! While it may be necessary to replace some of your furniture every couple of years—a new bed, mattress or dining room table, perhaps—do try to restrain yourself!

HOUSEHOLD HACKS
My top 8 hacks for purchasing furniture

☐ **Start buying second hand!** You can always give used items a thorough clean and wipe! Use sites such as Gumtree and Facebook Marketplace to connect with people wishing to offload their furniture. People moving house are often desperate to get rid of something, so they will advertise things such as furniture for free.

☐ **Keep an eye out for regular council 'hard rubbish' or 'household waste' collection days.** I regard these as just one big neighbourhood swap meet: you just have to hope it doesn't rain! It's recycling and saving at its very best. I once scored a sofa worth about $3000 for free from a neighbour moving interstate. I also have a lovely entertainment unit and bookcase I found this way.

- [ ] **You can also go further afield and check the local council websites of the more salubrious suburbs in your city for their collection dates.** You'd be surprised what wealthy people chuck out! By far my favourite find this way was a Georg Jensen clock retailing for more than $300 that just needed a wipe and a new battery. Rich people, huh?

- [ ] **Join local 'Street Bounty' Facebook groups in your area** where people post pictures of items left discarded on the street for other people to retrieve.

- [ ] **Join local 'Buy Nothing', 'Pay It Forward' or 'Buy, Swap, Sell' groups on Facebook.**

- [ ] **Time your purchases with sale periods such as Black Friday** for large discounts, if buying new furniture can't be avoided.

- [ ] **Join up to the retailer's email list when shopping online, then 'add to cart' and close your browser.** You'd be surprised how often stores will target you offering discounts if you simply walk away.

- [ ] **Always haggle by asking, 'What is the best price you can do on this?'** Make sure to smile! (This only works when buying in-store, obviously.)

	Weekly	Fortnightly	Monthly	Quarterly	Annually
Furniture					

Décor

Décor includes all the smaller household items you might buy to decorate your home, including:

- **indoor plants, candles, clocks, paintings, sculptures, ornaments, art (excluding art purchased as an investment)**

- **kitchenware such as glassware, tableware, cutlery, utensils, bakeware, crockery, containers, food wraps and shopping bags**

- **household linen such as bed sheets, blankets, doonas, pillows, cushions, towels, face washers, table linen and tea towels**

- **floor, window and light coverings; carpets, floor rugs and mats; vinyl and other sheet floor coverings; floor tiles; curtains and blinds.**

Note: I have put the cost of seasonal or holiday decorations—such as for Easter, Christmas and Halloween—under a later 'Lifestyle' category, as they are more discretionary in nature.

HOUSEHOLD HACKS
My top 2 hacks for not overspending on décor

I don't know who needs to hear this, but you are spending too much on décor. I know how tempting it is to hit up your local big box store and binge on cheap imported home décor. Don't do it!

- ☐ **Jump on Facebook Marketplace.** Use the 'search my local area' feature and change the maximum price for your search to $0. Then go score your freebie!

- ☐ **Take a list to the store and only buy the things on that list.** Easier said than done, I know. But try!

	Weekly	Fortnightly	Monthly	Quarterly	Annually
Décor					

Appliances

I guarantee you that one day your dishwasher or dryer is going to break down and you will need to replace it. It is one of life's 'known unknowns'. Don't be caught off guard; make sure you're aware of the potential costs involved in occasionally replacing your appliances, both big and small. It may be prudent to estimate an annual sum for replacing one or two big items and pop it in the 'Annually' column below.

Don't forget to think about both big and small appliances:

- *big appliances:* **stove, oven, fridge, freezer, dishwasher, air conditioner, washing machine, clothes dryer, vacuum cleaner, television, hot water system**
- *small appliances:* **toaster, kettle, microwave, hand mixer, coffee machine, blender, food mixer, rice cooker, hairdryer, electric shaver or trimmer, DVD player.**

A note on gadgets: I have put the cost of computers, laptops and tablets under a later 'Education' category. The cost of phone handsets goes under 'Utilities' with the cost of internet and phone plans. The cost of games consoles and other entertainment electronics goes under 'Lifestyle'.

HOUSEHOLD HACKS
My top hack for purchasing appliances

Don't fall victim to lifestyle inflation! Remember your worth as a person does not depend on having a $200 toaster to display on your counter top. When my kettle broke, I paid $5 for a still-in-the-box plastic one on Facebook Marketplace. And if you do want a fancy one, know that they often sell for half the price on Marketplace.

	Weekly	Fortnightly	Monthly	Quarterly	Annually
Appliances					

Home maintenance and repairs

If you're a home owner, you'll need to budget for minor repairs and maintenance to your property. It's one of the hidden costs of home ownership. Renters can be thankful their landlords usually pay for these things (and if they don't, push them because they can claim it as a tax deduction).

Costs to consider here include professional service expenses (plumbers, electricians, etc.) plus the cost of any DIY products you might buy at a hardware store. Think: painting, electrical work, plumbing, re-roofing, new fixtures such as doors, light switches, light globes, fire alarms, plaster, putty, new taps, nails, screws, hammers, other tools and batteries.

A note about major home renovations: Large, one-off home improvements that will definitely add dollars to your property's value go beyond maintenance and repair costs and might be better viewed as an investment saved for separately out of your budget surpluses, and not considered here as regular spending. Be careful though: home structures are actually depreciating assets and not everything you do—unless it's quite structural, like adding a bedroom—will be guaranteed to increase your home's sale price.

HOUSEHOLD HACKS

My top home-improvement hack

Avoid performing any major repair or renovation work for at least a year after moving into a new place. This obviously excludes emergency work to make the home habitable. When I first moved into my 1970s flat, I wanted to knock down a wall, move the kitchen, cover my vermiculite—aka 'popcorn'—ceiling, redo my floors and change all my light fittings. Instead, I lived with them all. They've grown on me and I reckon I've saved at least $50 000.

	Weekly	Fortnightly	Monthly	Quarterly	Annually
Home maintenance and repairs					

Cleaning

To truly make your house a home, you're going to want to keep it fresh and sparkling clean from top to bottom! In this sub-category, we consider the cost of all cleaning supplies and equipment for your home, including the kitchen, bathroom, laundry and the rest of the house — for example:

- *kitchen:* **dishwashing powder/tablets, dish brushes, sponges, scourers, wipes, paper towels, garbage bags, bin liners, mop, bucket, broom, dustpan and brush, general purpose cleansers, floor cleaners**
- *laundry:* **detergents, fabric softeners, stain removers, nappy disinfectant**
- *bathroom:* **air freshener, toilet cleaner, toilet brush, disinfectant bleach, window-cleaning products, unblocking agents**
- *other:* **shoe polishers, dusters, vacuum cleaner bags.**

How much you spend on such cleaning supplies will, of course, depend on the size of your household. In the year I tracked my spending, I spent $224 on cleaning supplies, mostly dishwashing and clotheswashing detergents. Make sure to include at least a small sum to cover these.

HOUSEHOLD HACKS
My top 6 cleaning hacks

☐ **Go natural!** Ditch your complicated array of household cleaners and stock up on bicarb, vinegar, lemons and citric acid (found in denture tablets!). Baking soda, or bicarb, is an alkaline that helps deodorise odours and vinegar is an acid that helps remove stains, mould and rust.

☐ **Microwave a cut lemon in a bowl of water to help lift stubborn stains in your microwave!**

☐ **To lift limescale from inside the kettle, mix half portions of water and vinegar and boil.**

- [ ] **Ditch single-use wipes!** You can pop microfibre cloths in the washing machine to extend their life.

- [ ] **Use much less detergent than you think you need for washing clothes.** Most people use way too much and it's not great for your clothes.

- [ ] **Use powdered dishwashing detergent** and use half the amount recommended. You'll be fine.

	Weekly	Fortnightly	Monthly	Quarterly	Annually
Cleaning					

Hygiene

Let's face it, there are certain standards of basic personal hygiene we should meet if we're going to function as part of a civil society. I don't think any house can be considered a home without providing supplies to keep its inhabitants from sweating and smelling, leaking and reeking …

For basic personal hygiene, estimate a cost for any of the following items that you might use: toilet paper, nappies, personal and baby wipes, sanitary products, tissues, toothbrushes and toothpaste, soap, body wash, shampoo, conditioner, deodorant, shaving cream, non–electric shavers and razors.

In a later category called 'Appearance' we'll tally the cost of items you buy that aren't really aimed at maintaining basic hygiene but at enhancing your appearance. These include things like fancy face creams, lotions, makeup and home beauty treatments. In the 'Health' category, we'll tally the cost of medically necessary personal care items like sunscreen, medical ointments, and contact lenses and solutions.

✅ HOUSEHOLD HACKS

My top 3 hygiene hacks

☐ **'Lather, rinse and repeat'** is one of the best marketing slogans ever invented. Halve your shampoo use by only shampooing once.

☐ **Use bar soaps, shampoos and conditioners**—they last longer.

☐ Ladies, **investigate period undies or menstrual cups**, which if you like them, might work out cheaper over time.

	Weekly	Fortnightly	Monthly	Quarterly	Annually
Hygiene					

Garden

Not everyone is living the backyard dream, but if you are, there are certain extra costs to consider, including the following: lawnmower, hedge cutter, outdoor furniture (if you haven't already budgeted for this in the 'Furniture' sub-category), barbecue, bottled gas, other fuels, trees, shrubs, plants, fertiliser, swimming pool chemicals, water pumps, wheelbarrows, watering cans, hoses, spades, secateurs, ladders and electric garden or power tools (either purchased or hired).

✔ HOUSEHOLD HACKS

My top 5 gardening hacks

- ☐ **Start composting your food scraps** for happy garden beds!

- ☐ **Get free mulch or discount composting bins.** Local councils sometimes offer them to encourage recycling. Check your local council website to find out more.

- ☐ **Join local gardening groups to swap seeds and cuttings.**

- ☐ **Take advantage of Bunnings' 'Perfect Plant Promise',** under which you can return any plant within 12 months for a full refund if it dies. The policy doesn't apply to seedlings and short-lived 'blooming' plants.

- ☐ **Scour Facebook Marketplace for garden supplies.** People often remodel their gardens and give away free pavers, landscaping rocks and plants.

	Weekly	Fortnightly	Monthly	Quarterly	Annually
Garden					

Strata fees

Also known as 'body corporate fees', these can be a substantial ongoing cost for owners of apartments, units and other 'strata title' buildings. These fees do, however, bundle together some of the costs that free-standing homeowners need to budget for separately. Strata fees can cover the cost of common area caretaking; gardening; stairwell cleaning; heating and lighting; maintenance of lifts, pools and refuse disposal chutes; building insurance; and some capital improvement works.

In addition to these regular fees, apartment owners should also be aware they may be up for additional levies imposed by strata committees (comprised of fellow owners) to cover any costs associated with remedial works and major building improvements or repairs.

✔️ **HOUSEHOLD HACKS**
My top 2 hacks for belonging to a body corporate

- [ ] **Request to see recent strata committee meeting notes,** annual reports and major capital works plans if you are looking to buy and apartment or unit. Look for discussion of any major building defects or upcoming works or levies. Make sure there is money in the 'sinking fund' for these, or you may be up for large unanticipated costs.

- [ ] **Join your strata committee to have your say, get to know your neighbours and work to minimise costs.** But it is a large time commitment.

	Weekly	Fortnightly	Monthly	Quarterly	Annually
Strata fees					

Home insurance

Lots of budgeting systems group together all insurances into one category called 'Insurance'. But I like to distribute them throughout my 10 budget categories according to the purpose of the insurance. Insuring your home against potential disasters, either natural or man-made, is a critical consideration for all homeowners.

Mortgage holders in free-standing homes are generally required by lenders to take out building and home insurance in their name to cover the cost of anything that goes wrong with the property. Strata owners should take care to check what repairs and replacements are covered by the building insurance policy and what needs to be insured separately.

Renters may also consider taking out contents insurance to cover the cost of replacing any stolen or damaged items.

HOUSEHOLD HACKS

My top 5 home insurance hacks

When it comes to insurance, you should always consider your own individual circumstances and preferences. But here are a few of my top ways to save on home insurance.

- ☐ **Don't just auto-renew every year.** Shop around to ensure you're still getting a competitive price.

- ☐ **Know that insurers offer their best prices to new customers, so consider becoming one.**

- ☐ **Use comparison sites** to compare premiums from multiple insurers.

(continued)

☐ **Consider a higher excess on your policy** (this is the amount you agree to pay out of your own pocket in the event of a claim). The higher the excess, the lower your ongoing premiums.

☐ **Don't own fancy things!** The higher the value of your belongings, the higher the amount you need to provide as an estimate of their value. The higher the sum insured, the higher your premiums. You end up paying double: once for the fancy thing and again—every year—to insure it!

	Weekly	Fortnightly	Monthly	Quarterly	Annually
Home insurance					

Council rates

Homeowners: welcome to another hidden cost of home ownership! Renters: relax; these costs are included in your rent.

Fees paid to local councils cover some pretty good stuff, like local parks, playgrounds and libraries. They also cover the cost of garbage disposal services and generally improve the neighbourhood facilities around you. Unavoidable, I'm afraid.

HOUSEHOLD HACKS

My top council rates saving hack

Local councils can offer a range of discounts, including an early payment discount if you pay on time, direct debit discounts and pensioner discounts. It's worth a phone call to find out if there are any ways to save. If you are in financial difficulty, ask about any 'financial hardship' provisions that may apply.

	Weekly	Fortnightly	Monthly	Quarterly	Annually
Council rates					

Household services

Sometimes it takes a village to look after your home and most of the time you have to pay them to do it. Here is a place to include any costs you incur for household services, including cleaners, gardeners, removalists, home help, carpet cleaners, pest exterminators, security services, locksmiths and private rubbish removal.

Note that statisticians have traditionally included nannies, au pairs and any other childcare services in this category. But given the importance of early learning, I include these in my 'Education' category. I include babysitting under 'Lifestyle' as it's usually associated with parents going out and having a bit of fun.

✔️ HOUSEHOLD HACKS

My top 3 household services savings hacks

☐ **Consider posting jobs around the home on a local Facebook group for your area or letter drop nearby streets.** Teenagers are an excellent source of cheap labour! My first job was mowing lawns.

☐ **Use sites such as Airtasker or hipages to find people to do odd jobs.**

☐ **Space out your appointments** (e.g. from weekly to fortnightly) for any regular service providers, such as cleaners.

	Weekly	Fortnightly	Monthly	Quarterly	Annually
Household Services					

• • •

And that's it; you're done with the 'Household' category! Did you fill out at least one number for every sub-category, even if it was '$0'? Did you calculate an annual figure for each? Well done you. I'm proud of you. Now let's connect your lovely home to essential services …

UTILITIES
Connect your home to essential services

This category covers a lot of things we usually take for granted, but definitely miss when they break down or get disconnected.

Utilities might sound boring, but the hint is right there in the name: 'utility' being the name given by economists to 'happiness' or 'wellbeing'.

While it's common to complain about utility bills, I think we should feel extremely grateful that we get to have these services at all.

Think about it.

How good is it you can turn your taps on and get fresh water freely flowing forth to drink and bathe yourself in?

How great is it that you have a toilet in your home and have your waste products magically whisked away to a local sewerage plant?

When it gets dark, how wonderful is it that you can just flick a switch and illuminate your home?

And there must be a name for that special existential angst and panic that descends if your internet gets disconnected. Traditionally, communication has been given a separate category from utilities such as electricity and gas, but I reckon in modern life, internet and phone are just as essential.

Essential services are often billed quarterly, or less regularly, so it's an important category to get you really thinking about those bigger costs that can derail your budgeting efforts.

Electricity

Historically, electricity suppliers were large, government-owned monopolies. But competition is hotting up. There has never been a better time to score a deal on your electricity.

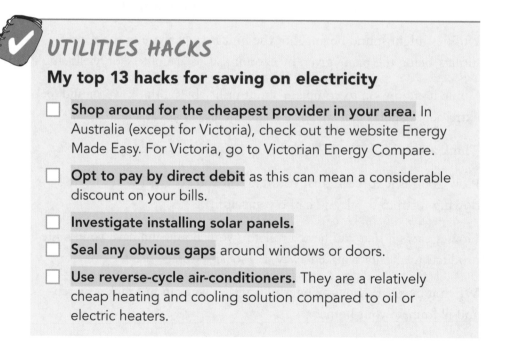

✔ UTILITIES HACKS

My top 13 hacks for saving on electricity

☐ **Shop around for the cheapest provider in your area.** In Australia (except for Victoria), check out the website Energy Made Easy. For Victoria, go to Victorian Energy Compare.

☐ **Opt to pay by direct debit** as this can mean a considerable discount on your bills.

☐ **Investigate installing solar panels.**

☐ **Seal any obvious gaps** around windows or doors.

☐ **Use reverse-cycle air-conditioners.** They are a relatively cheap heating and cooling solution compared to oil or electric heaters.

- [ ] **Turn your fridge down to the lowest setting**, particularly in winter.
- [ ] **Turn off appliances at the power point.**
- [ ] **Check the energy efficiency rating of your appliances**, particularly older fridges, which can be power hungry.
- [ ] **Switch to energy-efficient light bulbs.**
- [ ] **Put on a jumper and invest in woolly socks**—your mum was right!
- [ ] **Snuggle up underneath a rug when watching TV** instead of turning on the heater.
- [ ] **Dry your clothes using clothing racks**, not in the clothes dryer.
- [ ] **Wash your clothes on a cold cycle.**

	Weekly	Fortnightly	Monthly	Quarterly	Annually
Electricity					

Gas

If you have gas connected to your home, you'll find it's often a cheaper source of power than electricity.

UTILITIES HACKS

My top hack for saving on gas

Make sure to shop around separately for your gas and electricity providers. Don't assume that the same provider will be cheaper for both. You can use the same government websites mentioned earlier to shop around for plan prices.

	Weekly	Fortnightly	Monthly	Quarterly	Annually
Gas					

Water and sewerage

These services are still usually provided via a government monopoly, so you can't expect to get much choice on who supplies your water or treats your waste. You'll be billed a supply charge and usage fees. Landlords usually cover these costs for renters, though they may pass on usage charges.

Also include here the cost of any privately supplied septic tanks or other waste disposal services, which are more common in rural areas.

✔ UTILITIES HACKS

My top 5 hacks for saving water

- ☐ **Have shorter showers.** Turn on some music and set yourself a personal challenge to get in and out of the shower in one song. Don't cheat and choose 'November Rain' by Guns N' Roses because that one goes for nearly nine minutes. (How good is it though!)
- ☐ **Install water-efficient shower heads.**
- ☐ **Flush your toilet on half flush.**
- ☐ **Water your garden in the evening** when it's cooler so you lose less to evaporation.
- ☐ **Try planting hardy plants** such as lavender and succulents, which are not too thirsty.

	Weekly	Fortnightly	Monthly	Quarterly	Annually
Water and sewerage					

Internet

Internet plans just keep getting cheaper and cheaper, providing you with ever more data at faster speeds. If you haven't switched providers for a few years, it's definitely time to shop around.

Also include here the cost of any new equipment, such as modems or wi-fi routers and any cloud storage subscription charges.

✔ UTILITIES HACKS

My top 3 hacks for reducing internet charges

☐ **Visit the website Whistle Out for both internet and phone deals.**

☐ **Monitor your usage** to find out if you can switch to a smaller data plan.

☐ **Drop to a lower-speed plan to see if it can handle your needs.** If you're only sending a few emails and watching Netflix, you may not need a super-fast speed plan.

	Weekly	Fortnightly	Monthly	Quarterly	Annually
Internet					

Phone

Include here the cost of any landline and mobile phone plans for all members of your household. Also include here the cost of replacement handsets or smartphones. You may choose to split this cost over several years, including an annual contribution to this multi-year cost, depending on how often you update your phone.

Note: This is one place where you might have multiple bills or accounts for multiple family members to keep track of. Feel free to write notes in the margin to list them out separately! But bundle them together for a total estimate of phone expenses for your household in the space below. If you're using the spreadsheet from my website, you can add extra rows to list out individual family members' bills, if you wish.

UTILITIES HACKS

My top 3 hacks for reducing phone bills

☐ **Consider a pre-paid mobile plan for kids or heavy data users** who might incur charges for going over data limits on regular plans, which can come with hefty charges.

☐ **Use comparison websites to compare plan prices**, which have fallen dramatically in recent years. Be sure to price check at least once a year.

☐ **Do your sums** to figure out if lengthy contracts offering free handsets are better than purchasing a cheaper handset outright and shopping around for the lowest cost plan provider.

	Weekly	Fortnightly	Monthly	Quarterly	Annually
Phone					

Postal services

I'm told that some people still write letters by hand and send them by snail mail! While I find this hard to believe, if this is you, you'd better pop that cost in here. Of course, there's no way around postal charges if you need to send a package. In general, I say to add the cost of postage or delivery services onto the cost of whatever individual item you are having delivered or sending, such as gifts. But you can also create a small allowance here, if you like.

✔ UTILITIES HACKS

My top 2 postage hacks

☐ **Beware of free postage.** Don't be fooled by websites that offer free postage if you spend over a certain amount. If you don't actually need the other things, don't spend more! It's a false economy.

☐ **Batch your items.** If you order a lot of things from a particular retailer, try to wait until you have multiple items to order, so that you only pay one postage fee for delivery.

	Weekly	Fortnightly	Monthly	Quarterly	Annually
Postal services					

TRANSPORT
Get from A to B

Okay, we've spent quite a bit of time at home. Now let's get out and about!

My first car was an aqua-green Mazda 121 'bubble' car, which my older brother helped me buy second hand. It had a manual transmission and no air-conditioning. I owned it for many years before unfortunately being rear-ended in a highway accident. I was okay—thanks for asking!

Next up, I bought my mum and dad's old Toyota Corolla and drove it happily for several years. More recently, I upgraded to driving a brand spanking new Volkswagen Tiguan—paid for in cash, requiring no car loan. After a couple of years, I've discovered that European cars often come with big price tags for ongoing maintenance and replacement parts. Just one of the hidden costs to consider when buying a car. I wish I'd kept the Corolla, to be honest.

According to the Australian Bureau of Statistics, transport is the third biggest category of spending, after housing and food. You may be surprised when you add up what a large chunk transport costs eat out of your household budget.

For car owners, there's regular ongoing costs, such as petrol and tolls, alongside larger annual costs such as registration, insurance, roadside assist, drivers licence fees, servicing, repairs and parts.

For public transport users, those weekly costs can really add up too.

Include in this category the costs you incur for all vehicles you own, except for recreational vehicles such as campervans, caravans, trailers, planes and boats, which go under 'Lifestyle'. Be sure to include here any costs related to motorbikes, push bikes and scooters.

A quick note about holidays: only include the costs here of your regular trips—to work, to the shops and so on. Transport costs incurred in the course of taking a holiday will be included later in my 'Lifestyle' category.

You're doing so well, by the way! Keep at it!

Vehicle purchase

Cars are depreciating assets. The minute you drive them out of the car yard, they lose thousands of dollars. Many personal finance experts say you should only ever buy second-hand cars.

I'm not a purist. If a new car brings you true joy, I'll leave that up to you. Personally, if I had my time again, I wouldn't buy a new car. I also wouldn't buy a European car, but a cheaper Korean or Japanese model like a Toyota, Honda, Mitsubishi, Subaru or Mazda, because the ongoing running costs of parts and repairs are generally lower.

The Royal Auto Club of Victoria runs an annual survey of the cheapest and most expensive cars to buy and maintain in Australia. It shows that smaller cars are not only cheaper to buy, but incur lower ongoing costs in terms of maintenance and repairs.

✔ TRANSPORT HACKS

My top 7 car-purchase hacks

☐ **Buy the cheapest and smallest car your ego can afford.**

☐ **Consider not buying a car at all!** Ride a bike. Catch public transport. Use a service like GoGet to hire a car for the day or hour, or borrow a car from a friend or family member. You will save yourself thousands of dollars in ongoing costs a year!

☐ **Consider buying cars from family or friends** so you know the vehicle's history and how well it's been looked after.

☐ **Consider sharing a car** with a neighbour or family member.

☐ **Consider buying second hand**, including private sales and auction houses that specialise in second-hand, ex-government fleet vehicles—for example, Pickles Auctions or Grays Online. There are others.

☐ **Ask dealers about buying a former demonstration car** for low kilometres and a big discount.

☐ **Consider renting out your car when you're not using it** to offset your costs. Look at Car Next Door and Drive My Car. Be sure to consider any insurance implications.

Include in this table any provision you would like to make for saving up to buy a new car, motorbike or whatever your vehicle of choice may be.

	Weekly	Fortnightly	Monthly	Quarterly	Annually
Vehicle purchase					

Vehicle loan payments

Many personal finance experts will also tell you never to buy a vehicle that you can't pay for outright in cash. I'm a realist. For some people, this just might not be possible. But there are several traps to look out for when it comes to borrowing to buy a car or other vehicle.

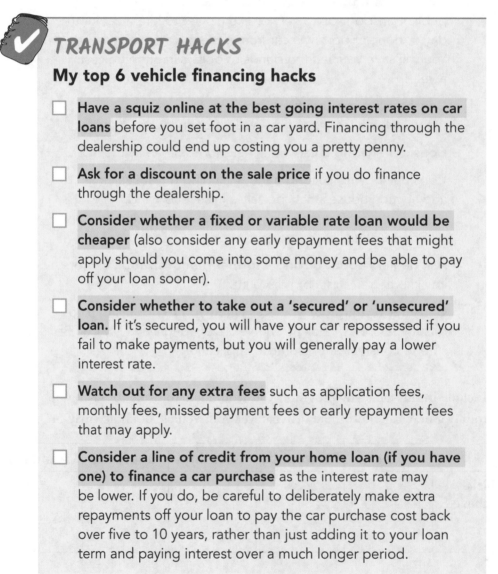

TRANSPORT HACKS
My top 6 vehicle financing hacks

☐ **Have a squiz online at the best going interest rates on car loans** before you set foot in a car yard. Financing through the dealership could end up costing you a pretty penny.

☐ **Ask for a discount on the sale price** if you do finance through the dealership.

☐ **Consider whether a fixed or variable rate loan would be cheaper** (also consider any early repayment fees that might apply should you come into some money and be able to pay off your loan sooner).

☐ **Consider whether to take out a 'secured' or 'unsecured' loan.** If it's secured, you will have your car repossessed if you fail to make payments, but you will generally pay a lower interest rate.

☐ **Watch out for any extra fees** such as application fees, monthly fees, missed payment fees or early repayment fees that may apply.

☐ **Consider a line of credit from your home loan (if you have one) to finance a car purchase** as the interest rate may be lower. If you do, be careful to deliberately make extra repayments off your loan to pay the car purchase cost back over five to 10 years, rather than just adding it to your loan term and paying interest over a much longer period.

	Weekly	Fortnightly	Monthly	Quarterly	Annually
Vehicle loan payments					

Vehicle registration

The first thing you need to do to get your vehicle on the road is ensure it is registered with the relevant authority. There's no getting around this one.

TRANSPORT HACKS

My top car rego hack

Pensioners and concession card holders are often entitled to discounted registration permits. In some states, tradespeople who use their vehicles for work are also entitled to a discount. It's always worth inquiring about discounts at your local motor vehicle registry.

	Weekly	Fortnightly	Monthly	Quarterly	Annually
Vehicle registration					

Drivers licence

You will also need a drivers licence. Generally these last a few years, but it's worth including a small annual provision for this cost.

✓ TRANSPORT HACKS

My top licence hack

Good drivers with no demerit points are eligible for a discount of 50 per cent in some states, so drive safely. Actually, just do that anyway!

	Weekly	Fortnightly	Monthly	Quarterly	Annually
Drivers licence					

Vehicle insurance

As part of paying your registration in Australia, you are obliged to purchase compulsory third-party insurance (CTP). This covers the cost of any disability you may cause to someone you hit in an accident.

It's also well worth considering what insurance you may need to cover the cost of any damage you might cause to other drivers' vehicles, or your own—particularly if you hit a Porsche!

There are a range of policy options available, so call a few insurers to discuss these. The rules for vehicle insurance are similar to home insurance: always shop around. Don't just auto-renew and consider a higher excess to reduce premiums.

TRANSPORT HACKS

My top 7 ways to save on vehicle insurance

☐ **Take advantage of low-mileage premiums.** If you don't drive much, be sure to let your insurer know because low-mileage drivers generally pay lower premiums.

☐ **Consider whether you really need comprehensive insurance.** In addition to the compulsory third-party insurance (which pays for the medical care of anyone you hurt in an accident), it's also possible to take out 'third party' policies that cover the cost of damaging another car (like that Porsche). Your car won't be covered, but if you have a cheap car, or if you could rely on family financial support to help you replace your car, it may not be worth paying a more expensive premium for comprehensive insurance.

☐ **Consider whether you want a 'market value' or 'agreed value' policy.** In the event of a total loss, a market value policy will pay you the open market value of your car at the time of a claim (remember that the value will fall as your car ages). An agreed value policy will pay out an agreed sum. I have mine set to a low agreed value, meaning I pay the

(continued)

lowest premium possible—I figure if I total my car, I'll just make do with a cheaper, second-hand one.

☐ **Don't pay for added windscreen insurance** if you can get this cover cheaper through your roadside assist provider. Worth checking.

☐ **Ask if there is a discount for paying annually**, rather than monthly.

☐ **Find out what discounts are available for bundling multiple policies**—home and contents with car insurance, for example—with one insurer. But also check that it's not cheaper to go with the cheapest insurer for each.

☐ **Compare CTP polices.** For residents of New South Wales, there is a government-run comparison site for CTP policies called 'Green Slip Price Search'.

	Weekly	Fortnightly	Monthly	Quarterly	Annually
Vehicle insurance					

Vehicle servicing and repairs

Ouch. This is where the cost of car ownership can really come back to bite you. Regular servicing is necessary to avoid bigger problems down the track.

✔ TRANSPORT HACKS

My top 5 hacks for keeping your vehicle on the road

☐ **Ask friends for recommendations** for reliable and affordable mechanics.

☐ **Confirm what's 'nice to have'.** A good mechanic should always be willing and able to explain to you the work they recommend on your car. If large repairs are recommended, ask whether they are necessary for your car's safety or just a 'nice to have' that could be done at the next service. Use your judgement. Get a second opinion if you feel unsure.

☐ **Cry poor!** I always complain to my mechanic how tight money is and how I can't afford anything that's not essential. It definitely seems to bring down the cost!

☐ **Consider spacing out your services if you can.** If you don't use your car very much, you may be able to get away with annual, rather than six-monthly, services. Talk to a trusted mechanic about this.

☐ **Teach yourself how to perform minor services** such as replacing oils and topping up necessary car bits. Honestly, I have no idea—but people do this, and it saves them money!

	Weekly	Fortnightly	Monthly	Quarterly	Annually
Vehicle servicing and repairs					

Vehicle parts and accessories

Some car parts need replacing every few years. Car batteries usually last between three and four years, and tyres about the same, depending on your mileage. Consider including a couple of hundred dollars a year in your annual budget to cover these irregular expenses.

This is also where those of you who choose to pimp your ride with a range of car accessories, including satellite navigation devices, dashboard cameras, roof racks, covers, snow chains, specialist hub caps or rims would enter your costs.

On a more practical note, parents and parents-to-be will need to budget for kids' car seats.

Bike riders are going to need helmets and other protective gear.

 TRANSPORT HACKS

My top 2 hacks for vehicle parts and accessories

☐ **Buy used or haggle on accessories.** Even though safety is paramount, it's still possible to purchase many of these items second hand. And if you do buy new, haggle hard!

☐ **Shop online to find great price deals on tyres**—you don't have to buy the ones your mechanic recommends. There are specialist online tyre retailers, and often more traditional retailers will have 'get the 4th tyre free' deals. Find your exact tyre size and specifications on the side of your tyres. My current size is 215/65 R16. That means three things. Firstly, my tyres are 215 millimetres wide. Secondly, the 'profile', or aspect ratio, of my tyres is 65. Thirdly, the diameter of my wheel rims is 16 inches. Punch your tyre details into Google to find some good deals.

	Weekly	Fortnightly	Monthly	Quarterly	Annually
Vehicle parts and accessories					

Roadside assist

If you don't have roadside assist, you can end up paying expensive call-out fees if you break down, your battery runs flat, you run out of petrol or you lock yourself out of your vehicle. I've always found it worth the cost for peace of mind.

TRANSPORT HACKS

My top roadside assistance hack

Consider what level of assistance you really need. Top-tier policies can pay for things like accommodation and transport if you break down, but base-level policies still give you peace of mind as you're covered for callouts.

	Weekly	Fortnightly	Monthly	Quarterly	Annually
Roadside assist					

Driving lessons

Oh, I remember those days! Vaguely …

TRANSPORT HACKS
My top driving lessons hack

Try to negotiate a discount for booking multiple sessions in advance.

	Weekly	Fortnightly	Monthly	Quarterly	Annually
Driving lessons					

Fuel

Filling up at the bowser is an unavoidable and ongoing cost of owning a car. Beyond simply not driving your car very much, there are other ways to be a savvy fuel shopper.

TRANSPORT HACKS
My top 5 hacks for saving on fuel costs

☐ **Use petrol price comparison apps to find the cheapest stations in your area and monitor the weekly price cycle.** In New South Wales, head to Fuel Check. In Victoria, there's the RACV Fuel Prices site. For everywhere else in Australia, there are national sites such as Gas Buddy, Petrol Spy and Motor Mouth.

☐ **Lock it in.** The 7/11 app has a 'price lock' feature that allows you to search for the cheapest 7/11 pump prices in your area and lock in a price to use at any 7/11 station over the coming seven days. Great for when you see pump prices are climbing.

☐ **Be aware of when petrol prices are about to rise or fall.** Search 'ACCC and petrol price cycles' online to find an Australian Competition and Consumer Commission webpage which shows you recent price movements in each capital city and advises whether you should wait to buy.

☐ **'Top up, don't fill up'** if you happen to find yourself running on empty when prices are at a peak.

☐ **Skip paying for expensive premium fuels** if your car manufacturer hasn't specified they're needed for your car. There will usually be a sticker inside your fuel flap specifying what octane rating fuel is required.

	Weekly	Fortnightly	Monthly	Quarterly	Annually
Fuel					

Tolls

Road tolls are an often unavoidable feature of modern life. But there are ways to save.

✔ TRANSPORT HACKS

My top 3 road-toll hacks

☐ **Make sure your beeper is correctly installed on your window**—and check that it beeps every time, because sometimes you'll pay an extra fee it if doesn't register.

☐ **Make sure you're signed up to any government 'cash back' schemes** that apply if you're a regular toll user.

☐ **Car pool with colleagues**, if you can, to avoid paying multiple tolls each.

	Weekly	Fortnightly	Monthly	Quarterly	Annually
Tolls					

Parking

Include here a provision for casual parking, if that's a likely expense for you, and the cost of any longer-term leases on car parking spaces. And don't forget to include an allowance for parking fines (you never know!).

✔ TRANSPORT HACKS

My top 4 parking hacks

☐ **Think ahead.** Big commercial car parking stations often offer discounts for booking online in advance.

☐ **Check out the Parkhound website for longer-term parking spaces**

☐ **Choose wisely.** Many of the larger chains also have websites that allow you to search for cheaper stations in your area.

☐ **Be prepared to park a bit further away from your destination**—you may save money and get fitter!

	Weekly	Fortnightly	Monthly	Quarterly	Annually
Parking					

Public transport

How much do you spend on fares for the bus, train, ferry or tram? These costs can really add up.

✓ TRANSPORT HACKS

My top public transport hack

Off-peak discounts often apply for travelling outside of morning and evening rush hours. Depending on your employer, you may be able to start or finish work early to avoid peak prices.

	Weekly	Fortnightly	Monthly	Quarterly	Annually
Public transport					

Vehicle hire, taxis and ride shares

Finally (phew!), include here an estimate of the costs you incur driving in other people's cars, be it a taxi, ride share, peer-to-peer rental or hiring a car. If you're on holidays, you should include these costs as part of your holiday budget under 'Lifestyle'.

TRANSPORT HACKS
My top driving costs hack

Consider being the 'designated driver' for your next night out. Your friends will love you and you'll save on both alcohol and late night taxis.

	Weekly	Fortnightly	Monthly	Quarterly	Annually
Vehicle hire, taxis and ride shares					

•••

Well done—you're really motoring through these categories! Remember to highlight a line across any expenses you have filled out, using your assigned colours, and always tally an annual cost.

Now it's time to tackle your food bills …

FOOD
Nourish your body

Ah, as Oliver once famously sang: 'Food, glorious food, what wouldn't we give for?'

Food eats large chunks out of all household budgets—particularly for those on lower incomes. Overall, it is the second biggest expense for the average Aussie household, after housing.

But I want to be super clear about what I mean by 'food'.

Firstly, I'm not simply talking about 'groceries', or whatever you spent at the supermarket. Household items such as nappies, shampoo, cleaning supplies and homewares should be tallied separately and categorised under 'Household' (it's a good idea to keep receipts and highlight these expenses using your coloured highlighters so you can track your spending by item).

My definition of food for this category is 'the cost of edible items you buy and use to prepare meals at home to fuel your body'.

To give you a picture of what's included, on the next page is a table showing some of the major food groups captured by the Australian Bureau of Statistics' household survey—basically, all the things you can buy in the store that would fit in my 'Food' category.

Proteins	Fats	Carbohydrates
beef	milk	bread
lamb	cream	flour
pork	cheese	cakes and puddings
chicken	butter	biscuits
fish and other seafood	yoghurt	breakfast cereals
ham	oils	pasta
bacon	nuts	rice
sausages	avocado	fresh fruit
eggs		fresh vegetables
		dried fruit
		sugar
		jams and honey
		potato crisps
Other		confectionary
tea and coffee		ice-cream
all non-alcoholic beverages		spices and herbs
baby food and formula		sauces
pet food		soft drinks
pre-packaged meals		fruit juices

Don't include here the cost of food or drinks you buy in a restaurant, pub or café, or from a takeaway food store, drive through, Uber Eats or other meal delivery service. They're listed later in the 'Lifestyle' category. As are all those takeaway coffees!

Why? Because in those instances, you are consuming both a good—that is, food or drink—and a service—that is, the cost of paying the wages of whoever prepared and delivered the food for you.

By far the best way to save money on food bills is to make sure you are only paying for the raw ingredients and not for the service involved in having someone else prepare, cook and serve them for you.

Any alcohol you consume—either at home or at a venue—also goes in the 'Lifestyle' category (which will be a really fun category, by the way, when we get to it!).

It's important to include in your food budget the total cost of feeding all your family members—including the furry ones. People often categorise pet expenses separately, but I get you to treat pets just like any other member of the family. Their food costs go under 'Food'. Their health costs, such as vet fees, come later under 'Health'.

Really, the only way to get a good estimate of your total food spend is by tracking your actual spending for a while. We'll look at how you can do this using my Spending Tracker worksheet in chapter 8. Once you see what you actually spend in, say, one month, you can set yourself a goal to lower it the next month, if you choose. For your reference, I currently spend $400 to $450 a month to feed myself and my young son (who lives with me for half of the week).

Put your best guess in the table. I really do urge you to just write anything —it's like taking your weight loss 'before' photo. At some point, you'll be able to look back with pride at how far you've come in really getting to know your food spending habits.

	Weekly	Fortnightly	Monthly	Quarterly	Annually
Food					

All right, now let's trim those food bills!

FOOD HACKS

My top 30 food hacks

At home:

☐ **Cook at home as much as you can**; that way you're not paying for the labour involved in someone else doing it for you.

☐ **Avoid waste.** Seriously, the best way to save on food is not to pay for the pleasure of chucking it in the bin.

☐ **Make friends with your freezer!** Check expiry dates and freeze or cook up food that's about to go 'off'.

☐ **Know the difference between 'use by' and 'best before' dates.** 'Use by' is a sign that the food manufacturer really thinks the food will not be edible after that date. 'Best before' means the quality may not be as good after the date, but it's still edible. If in doubt, use your nose and give it a sniff!

☐ **Shop your pantry first.** You'd be surprised how long you can last without restocking. Set yourself a challenge to last as long as you can before you need to go to the shops to buy more food.

☐ **Write out a pantry inventory.** I did once and had about $500 of food sitting there.

☐ **Write the price of everything you buy on the packaging with a big black marker.** It reminds you you're wasting money if you throw it away!

☐ **Eat what you buy.** The best way to organise your pantry is to eat it! I know we're all obsessed with home pantry storage and organisation, but seriously, make sure you eat it.

- [ ] **Download the SuperCook app.** It has a handy function which spits out a list of possible recipes based on the ingredients you have, allowing you to use up your leftovers.

- [ ] **Pull out the salad drawer in your fridge** altogether—it's a graveyard for fruit and veg.

- [ ] **Place fruit and veg and food items you need to consume soon on the most accessible shelf in the fridge.**

- [ ] **Wash and pre-chop your vegetables** so they are ready to grab and go.

- [ ] **Go meatless for a few meals a week.**

- [ ] **Bulk out your meat recipes with legumes.** For example, try adding a tin of lentils to a spaghetti bolognaise.

- [ ] **Pre-cook your meats and store them in your freezer** in individually portioned, meal-sized servings so you can grab, defrost and devour them.

- [ ] **Roast trays of vegetables on a Sunday**—everything tastes better roasted! My personal faves are capsicum, cauliflower, pumpkin and sweet potato.

- [ ] **Pre-make in bulk.** My favourite meals to cook in batches over the weekend and whip out on weeknights are bolognaise sauce (cook spaghetti on the night), mince fried in Moroccan spice (add to salads), tuna mornay (kids love it) and sausages (pre-cooked).

- [ ] **Grow some veggies.**

- [ ] **Pack your work lunches from home**—you really don't need me to tell you that one!

(continued)

FOOD

- [ ] **Follow my 'rule of three' for eating.** Look back at the table of foods on page 128. Grab a protein, grab a fat and grab a carb and *boom*: you've got yourself a meal.

In store:

- [ ] **Try the 'GST' diet.** Buy mostly fresh veggies and meats and you will avoid paying the extra tax that applies to pre-packaged foods.

- [ ] **Watch the bottom shelves.** Supermarkets put their highest profit margin items at eye height, so get down low to score a better deal.

- [ ] **Give home-brand products a try.** Honestly, we live in a rich nation—even our lowest quality products would be a banquet in some other countries.

- [ ] **Always look for 'per unit' pricing** to help you find the cheapest products.

- [ ] **Buy in bulk** when your regular items are on sale.

- [ ] **Download apps like Wiselist, frugl and Half Price.** These apps search competing grocery chains to find the cheapest prices and the best weekly specials on individual items.

- [ ] **Don't take kids shopping with you**, if you can possibly avoid it. Trust me.

- [ ] **Don't shop when you're hungry.**

- [ ] **Take a list and only buy the things on it.** I know—revolutionary, right?

- [ ] **Buy frozen berries and defrost them** as this can be much cheaper, especially out of season.

Another category completed—congratulations! Let's move on to your health now.

HEALTH
Prevent and cure illness

Health is one of my most important values. I like to spend money in ways that enhance my physical and mental health.

I include preventative spending in my health category: this includes gym memberships and sports fees. I actually view such expenses as investments in my future income-earning capacity.

Private health insurance, of course, is a major cost for many families. Premiums have risen massively in recent years, and I have listed below my top ways to shave premiums. Even private health insurance, however, doesn't cover you for everything, and it's important for everyone to budget for unexpected medical expenses.

Include here the medical costs for all your family members, including pet insurance, registration and vet fees for your furry, scaly or feathery household members.

Health insurance

In Australia, if you earn over the income threshold to pay the Medicare levy surcharge (currently $90 000 for singles and $180 000 for couples), it's well worth looking at taking out an eligible health cover policy to save at tax time. There are some basic hospital policies that cost less than the tax surcharge would cost you.

HEALTH HACKS

My top 10 health-insurance hacks

☐ **Only get cover for 'extras' if you can actually see you will receive more in claim benefits than you will pay out in premiums.** You're only required to have eligible hospital cover (not extras cover) to avoid paying the Medicare levy surcharge.

☐ **Make sure to use up your extras benefits (if you get them) before they reset each year**, usually at the start of the year.

☐ **Consider pre-paying your annual premiums** ahead of regular price hikes, which usually occur in April. This locks you in to pay the older, lower price.

☐ **Consider increasing your excess**—the amount you agree to pay out of pocket in the event of a claim—to reduce your ongoing premiums. Currently the maximum excess allowable is $750 for singles policies and $1500 for families.

☐ **Don't pay for cover you don't need.** If you're young and healthy, you may not need to pay for cover for joint replacements and weight loss reduction surgery.

☐ **Mums, don't forget to drop obstetrics from your cover** once you're done having kids.

☐ **Be aware of the Lifetime Health Cover (MHC) loading**, which applies if you don't take out a health-insurance policy before you turn 30 and keep it after the age of 30. But also calculate, if you don't currently need insurance, if it might actually be cheaper to pay the higher loading should you need insurance in the future. Do your research and your own sums.

- [ ] **Be aware you can have up to three years without cover after you're 30 without incurring the loading.** This can include multiple periods that add up to a maximum of three years.

- [ ] **Be aware of the 'mental health waiver'**, which means that even if you have restricted cover for 'psychiatric' conditions, everyone is allowed a once-in-a-lifetime opportunity to upgrade their cover, should they need to, to a higher level without serving a two-month waiting period. This waiver can only be used once. And you must have already served any waiting periods on your existing cover. But if losing access to full psychiatric cover is a major concern in switching to a cheaper policy, this is something worth knowing.

- [ ] **Use comparison sites to look for cheaper deals.** But beware: some policies may look cheaper on the surface, but don't provide the same coverage. Make sure you're comparing like-for-like and any new policy covers you for everything you want.

	Weekly	Fortnightly	Monthly	Quarterly	Annually
Health insurance					

Pet insurance and veterinary costs

Include here all the costs of keeping your fur babies in tip-top health condition. Include premiums for any pet insurance plus an estimate of likely out-of-pocket veterinary charges on things such as de-sexing, vaccinations, de-worming tablets and tick and flea treatments.

As with any insurance, you can choose to 'self-insure' for your pet's health costs if you have enough savings put aside. Some breeds do, however, come with higher health risks. Investigate your options. Some people swear by pet insurance and others don't get much value from it.

This is also where you can factor in any local council pet registration fees or micro-chipping charges.

If you're buying a pet, the costs come under 'Lifestyle' in a sub-category I call … you guessed it … 'Pet purchases'!

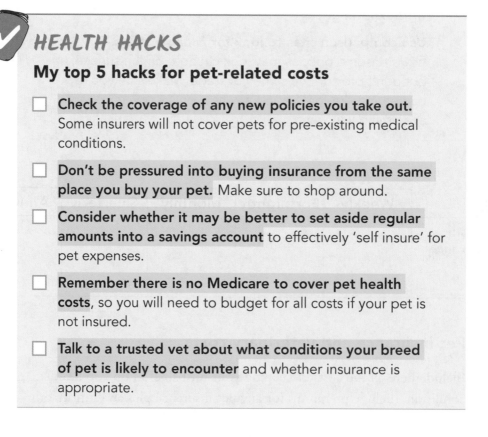

✔ HEALTH HACKS

My top 5 hacks for pet-related costs

☐ **Check the coverage of any new policies you take out.** Some insurers will not cover pets for pre-existing medical conditions.

☐ **Don't be pressured into buying insurance from the same place you buy your pet.** Make sure to shop around.

☐ **Consider whether it may be better to set aside regular amounts into a savings account** to effectively 'self insure' for pet expenses.

☐ **Remember there is no Medicare to cover pet health costs**, so you will need to budget for all costs if your pet is not insured.

☐ **Talk to a trusted vet about what conditions your breed of pet is likely to encounter** and whether insurance is appropriate.

	Weekly	Fortnightly	Monthly	Quarterly	Annually
Pet insurance and veterinary costs					

Doctors and specialists

Being able to pay for and access proper medical care when you need it is one of the most important things you can plan for. Include here the costs of any likely annual or more regular trips to the following: GP, physiotherapist, rehab, chiropractor, dermatologist, gynaecologist, IVF, radiology, podiatrist, psychologist and any other mental health support.

Budget only for the out-of-pocket cost you will pay—that is, after any Medicare or health insurance rebates have been factored in.

HEALTH

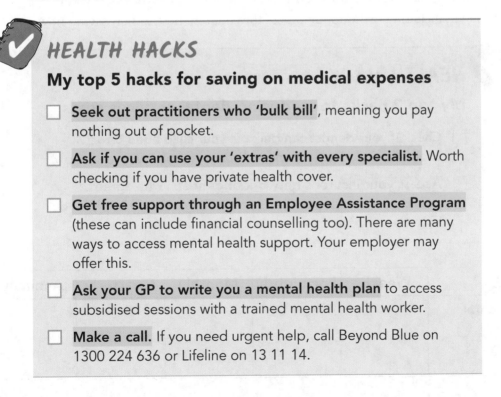

HEALTH HACKS

My top 5 hacks for saving on medical expenses

☐ **Seek out practitioners who 'bulk bill'**, meaning you pay nothing out of pocket.

☐ **Ask if you can use your 'extras' with every specialist.** Worth checking if you have private health cover.

☐ **Get free support through an Employee Assistance Program** (these can include financial counselling too). There are many ways to access mental health support. Your employer may offer this.

☐ **Ask your GP to write you a mental health plan** to access subsidised sessions with a trained mental health worker.

☐ **Make a call.** If you need urgent help, call Beyond Blue on 1300 224 636 or Lifeline on 13 11 14.

	Weekly	Fortnightly	Monthly	Quarterly	Annually
Doctors and specialists					

Dental

Be sure to budget for at least an annual dental check-up and clean to keep your pearly whites bright and to avoid any nasty bigger surprises down the track. Depending on your level of cover, some people with Extras health insurance may still need to pay out-of-pocket charges for excluded items, such as fillings and x-rays. Check your policy to see what you are covered for.

Parents, take a moment to consider any future orthodontic fees you may incur, including orthodontic braces for children. Best to start saving now.

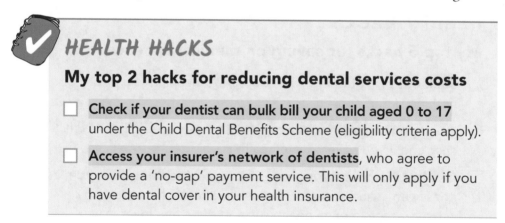

HEALTH HACKS

My top 2 hacks for reducing dental services costs

☐ **Check if your dentist can bulk bill your child aged 0 to 17** under the Child Dental Benefits Scheme (eligibility criteria apply).

☐ **Access your insurer's network of dentists**, who agree to provide a 'no-gap' payment service. This will only apply if you have dental cover in your health insurance.

	Weekly	Fortnightly	Monthly	Quarterly	Annually
Dental					

HEALTH

Optical

Four-eyes and contact-lens wearers alike face the added cost of keeping their eyesight 20:20. Health insurance Extras policies generally cover some, but not all, costs.

	Weekly	Fortnightly	Monthly	Quarterly	Annually
Optical					

Hospital and ambulance

Include here the cost of any services provided in a private hospital that are not covered by insurance, such as a private obstetrician or anaesthetist (I nearly kissed mine when I got my epidural), plus ambulance charges (if you are not insured). This may not be something you can actually estimate. Just be aware that costs can arise. Mostly, we should be thankful to live in a country with great public hospital care.

Do be aware, however, that ambulance trips aren't covered by Medicare. You can be charged both a call-out fee and a per-kilometre fee. Queenslanders and Tasmanians are the only exception, as your state government picks up the tab. For the rest, consider whether you want to take out cover through your health insurer, and ask them whether they cover the full cost of an ambulance trip—you might have to take out ambulance membership as well to be fully covered.

	Weekly	Fortnightly	Monthly	Quarterly	Annually
Hospital and ambulance					

Medicines

Include here all the products you buy that have a medicinal quality or protect your health, such as regular drugs (both prescription and non-prescription), sunscreen, vitamins, contraceptives, condoms and lubricants. Also consider vaccination costs here.

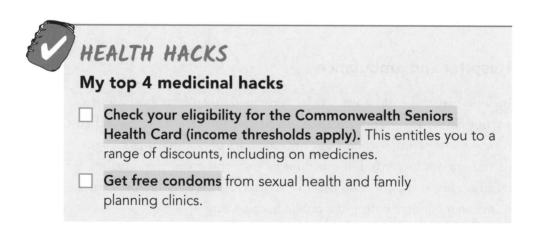

✔ HEALTH HACKS

My top 4 medicinal hacks

☐ **Check your eligibility for the Commonwealth Seniors Health Card (income thresholds apply).** This entitles you to a range of discounts, including on medicines.

☐ **Get free condoms** from sexual health and family planning clinics.

- [ ] **Ask your GP if they have any freebies.** Sometimes pharmaceutical companies give doctors samples to try.

- [ ] **Be sure to keep your medicines cupboard or box well organised** so you don't buy too much of the same thing. And regularly check expiry dates.

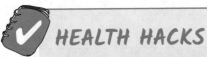

	Weekly	Fortnightly	Monthly	Quarterly	Annually
Medicines					

Medical equipment

Think of all the first-aid supplies you might need to keep on hand, including bandaids, dressings, bandages, thermometers, pregnancy tests and icepacks.

When considering future retirement needs, be aware you may require more equipment to aide your mobility and daily living when you're older, including therapeutic footwear, hearing aids, walking frames, wheelchairs, sticks and canes, chairs for showering, hand rails, ramps, pressure relief mattresses and special beds.

✔ HEALTH HACKS

My top medical supplies hack

First-aid kits usually come with a bunch of stuff you'll never need. Save money by creating your own. Ask your doctor what to include.

	Weekly	Fortnightly	Monthly	Quarterly	Annually
Medical equipment					

Sport and fitness

Finally, the fun bit of this category!

Include here the cost of all the preventative work you do to keep your body flexible and fit, including gym, health and fitness membership charges, wearable fitness technology, sporting club fees (ones where you actually do sports, not just spectate), sports lessons and hire of sporting facilities, including courts and green fees.

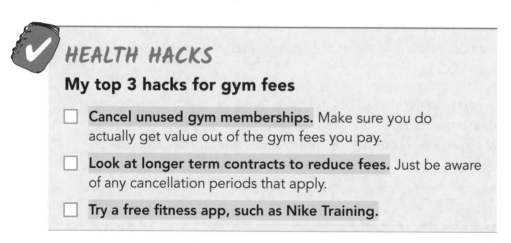

HEALTH HACKS
My top 3 hacks for gym fees

- [ ] **Cancel unused gym memberships.** Make sure you do actually get value out of the gym fees you pay.
- [ ] **Look at longer term contracts to reduce fees.** Just be aware of any cancellation periods that apply.
- [ ] **Try a free fitness app, such as Nike Training.**

	Weekly	Fortnightly	Monthly	Quarterly	Annually
Sport and fitness					

EDUCATION
Acquire knowledge to boost future income

Like health, education is an area where I give myself the green light to spend. Money invested on expanding your knowledge can improve your future income-earning capacity.

Most obviously, this category includes school fees and other costs such as uniforms and excursions. It also includes higher education and the cost of any professional or continuing education. Don't forget to tax deduct these, where applicable.

Home computing devices such as desktop computers, laptops and tablets also go here (smartphones are covered under 'Utilities'). Yes, I know these devices can also be used for entertainment, but they're essential if you want to stay up to date in the workforce these days.

I also budget all childcare costs under this category, with studies having shown the importance of early learning. For ease, I include nannies, au pair and after-school-care costs here too. Babysitting that is mainly so parents can go out and have fun is listed under 'Lifestyle'.

Those of us with an addiction to stationery get to include it here as this no doubt makes us very educated and clever people (just don't go overboard, okay?).

Books, newspapers and magazines

Books, and newspaper and magazine subscriptions kick off this category. Yes, you have my green light to devour books and subscribe to your favourite newspapers. Include subscriptions to online services such as Audible.

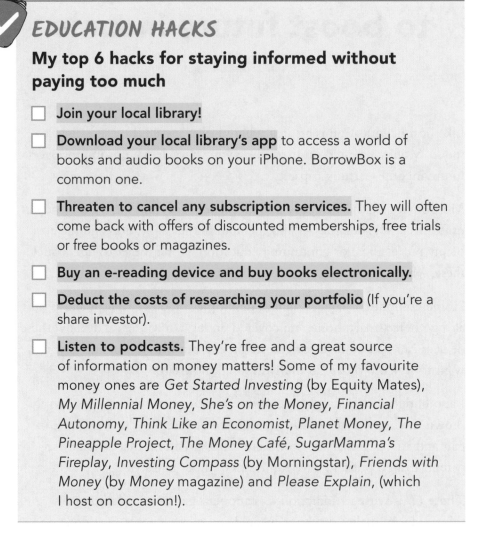

✔ EDUCATION HACKS

My top 6 hacks for staying informed without paying too much

- ☐ **Join your local library!**

- ☐ **Download your local library's app** to access a world of books and audio books on your iPhone. BorrowBox is a common one.

- ☐ **Threaten to cancel any subscription services.** They will often come back with offers of discounted memberships, free trials or free books or magazines.

- ☐ **Buy an e-reading device and buy books electronically.**

- ☐ **Deduct the costs of researching your portfolio** (If you're a share investor).

- ☐ **Listen to podcasts.** They're free and a great source of information on money matters! Some of my favourite money ones are *Get Started Investing* (by Equity Mates), *My Millennial Money*, *She's on the Money*, *Financial Autonomy*, *Think Like an Economist*, *Planet Money*, *The Pineapple Project*, *The Money Café*, *SugarMamma's Fireplay*, *Investing Compass* (by Morningstar), *Friends with Money* (by *Money* magazine) and *Please Explain*, (which I host on occasion!).

	Weekly	Fortnightly	Monthly	Quarterly	Annually
Books, newspapers and magazines					

Stationery

Pens, paper, diaries, planners, envelopes, printing and photocopying—pop 'em all in here.

✓ EDUCATION HACKS

Top money saving hack for stationery

Remember to claim a tax deduction for the cost of any stationery you use in the course of performing your work duties and for which your employer has not already reimbursed you. Keep receipts.

	Weekly	Fortnightly	Monthly	Quarterly	Annually
Stationery					

Home computer equipment

Even if you don't actually buy a new one every year, it can be useful to allow for the cost of buying new laptops, desktop computers, tablets and other devices over multiple years. Don't forget the cost of accessories such as monitors, printers and software. Games and gaming equipment go in the 'Lifestyle' category.

EDUCATION

✔️ EDUCATION HACKS

My top 3 home computer purchase hacks

☐ **Ask for a student discount on technology.** If you're a student, ask your technology provider for a discount.

☐ **Investigate 'refurbished' or second-hand computers.** Just make sure they're from a reputable dealer.

☐ **Don't catch 'upgrade-itis'.** Find out whether you really need the latest upgrade or whether your older model will do just fine.

	Weekly	Fortnightly	Monthly	Quarterly	Annually
Home computer equipment					

Childcare

Include your out-of-pocket costs (after government subsidies) for all centre-based childcare, family day care, preschool costs and after-school care. Also include costs for a nanny or au pair service.

✔️ EDUCATION HACKS

My top childcare hack

Make sure you're registered to receive any government support and rebates available.

	Weekly	Fortnightly	Monthly	Quarterly	Annually
Childcare					

School

Parents of school-aged kids—both primary and secondary—buckle up! This is the place for parents who send their kids to private schools to add their tuition fees. Public schools can also charge annual fees to cover textbooks, excursions and other costs.

Uniform costs can really add up because the kids just keep on outgrowing their uniforms. Also include costs for excursions, sports, music and dance lessons, private tuition fees, textbooks, school photos, arts supplies, stationery, lunchboxes and drink bottles and, last but not least, end-of-year teacher presents. We love you guys!

✔ EDUCATION HACKS

My top school-costs hack

Make friends with parents at your school who have children in older years and score some hand-me-down uniforms, bags or textbooks! Also, you get a new friend!

	Weekly	Fortnightly	Monthly	Quarterly	Annually
School					

Higher education

Investing in yourself through higher education can pay off later in life in the way of higher earnings. Include here all student loan repayments, higher education institution fees, TAFE course fees and fees for other education courses.

In Australia, student loans under the Higher Education Loan Program (HELP) only have to be repaid once you're in the workforce and earning above certain income thresholds. At that point, compulsory repayments will be deducted.

Students also have the option of making voluntary repayments, but I recommend you consider this carefully as HELP loans are perhaps the best loan you will ever get. You pay no interest on the amount owning, with outstanding loan amounts simply indexed to inflation. And there's no date by which you have to repay the loan.

If you're in the workforce, include the cost of professional development courses and continuing education.

EDUCATION

EDUCATION HACKS
My top higher-education-costs hack

Many TAFEs offer free courses, subsidised by government. It's worth inquiring about what may be available.

	Weekly	Fortnightly	Monthly	Quarterly	Annually
Higher education					

APPEARANCE

Influence how other people see you

If you wax it, pluck it, groom it or bleach it, it goes here.

I want you to know I think you're perfect just as you are. I wouldn't change a thing about you.

Unfortunately, the way you appear has been shown by numerous studies to influence your income-earning capacity.

So here we tally up all the other costs involved in maintaining your appearance, or how other people see you.

You'll need clothes, of course—the alternative being somewhat frowned upon by the law.

Then it's up to you how much you choose to spend on the dazzling array of adornments and beauty treatments available these days.

Ladies, I'm only going to say this once: you're already staring down the barrel of a fairly substantial income gap in retirement, given the likelihood you will not be paid the same as your male colleagues or will take time out from the workforce to have and raise children. Do you really want to make that financial gap even worse by dropping thousands of dollars a year on beauty treatments? Sermon over.

Enter grooming costs for your entire household, including the hairier ones, like pets (but not exclusively pets …).

Remember, we already included the cost of basic hygiene items, such as shampoo, deodorant and toothpaste, in the 'Household' category. Sunscreen and anything medicinal—designed to treat medical conditions—should also have been included in your 'Health' category.

Clothes and shoes

One year, I just didn't buy any clothes. It is possible, people. Since then, I've discovered the joys of buying clothes second hand. Include here an annual estimate of what you spend, including the cost of any dry cleaning, laundering, clothing hire and repairs and alterations.

APPEARANCE HACKS

My top 11 hacks for saving on clothes and shoes

- [ ] **Shop at op shops, thrift shops and charity shops** and buy second hand.
- [ ] **Volunteer at the same shops** and you get first pick!
- [ ] **Haggle on price at charity shops.** It's okay, just be really nice. It's a charity, after all.
- [ ] **Try a 'no-spend' year for clothes.**
- [ ] **Shop in the kids' clothes section** if you're on the smaller side of things—it's cheaper!
- [ ] **Search Facebook Marketplace** for kids' clothes to find bundles in your child's next size.

- ☐ **Handwash silk with wool wash**, towel dry and hang in the shade instead of dry cleaning.
- ☐ **Search for 'consignment' sellers**, who sell high-end second-hand clothes on consignment via Instagram or websites.
- ☐ **Join a clothes subscription service** such as Glam Corner to replenish your work wardrobe each month.
- ☐ **Rent outfits for one-off events** rather than purchasing them new.
- ☐ **Consider the 'cost per wear'.** If you do buy new clothes, sometimes cheaper items don't last as long. But also don't use this as an excuse to overpay!

	Weekly	Fortnightly	Monthly	Quarterly	Annually
Clothes and shoes					

Accessories

I'm talking hats, handbags, belts, sunglasses, jewellery, cufflinks, watches, ties, scarves and gloves. Really, you can do without these too. But you do you!

APPEARANCE HACKS
My top accessories hack

Claim handbags on tax! The Australian Tax Office lets you claim the value of one handbag or briefcase that you use for work purposes worth less than $300 each year. Get on it.

	Weekly	Fortnightly	Monthly	Quarterly	Annually
Accessories					

Hairdressing

I remember in my first application for a loan, I specified I would need to spend $1250 a year for hair treatments consisting of two appointments for a full head of foils ($405 each), two appointments for just a T–section of foils ($175) and $90 to get my boy shorn a couple of times a year. How I've changed! I haven't spent a cent on a professional hairdresser for myself for almost two years. Friends, it's possible to live differently!

Don't forget to include grooming costs for pets here too.

APPEARANCE HACKS
My top 4 hairdressing hacks

- [ ] **Cut your own hair!** Get a sharp pair of scissors or clippers and off you go!

- [ ] **Get a friend to cut your hair!** Make sure you pick a friend you would willingly take a bullet for. This way you know your friendship will endure, regardless, and that they'll have a deeply vested interest in doing a good job.

- [ ] **Ask local salons or TAFEs about training days** for discounted services.

- [ ] **Space out your appointments:** if you usually go every eight weeks, try 10 weeks instead.

	Weekly	Fortnightly	Monthly	Quarterly	Annually
Hairdressing					

Beauty products

These are all the products that transcend my definition of providing 'basic personal hygiene'. That's makeup, non-essential and non-medicinal skin lotions and treatments, and fragrances. You're of course allowed to spend your money on these things. Just try to keep it under control.

APPEARANCE HACKS
My top 2 beauty products hacks

☐ **Try cheaper products/brands** just to see if they achieve the same thing for you.

☐ **Stock up on your favourite products** at supermarkets when they are half price.

	Weekly	Fortnightly	Monthly	Quarterly	Annually
Beauty products					

Beauty treatments

Wow! There are just so many these days: hair removal, facials, microdermabrasion, laser treatments, waxing, needling, eyebrow sculpting and colouring, lash tints, depilation, pedicures, manicures, saunas, non-medical massages, tattoo and piercing services …

APPEARANCE HACKS
My top 2 hacks for beauty treatments

☐ **Space out your appointments** or bulk buy these treatments when they're on special.

☐ **Ask yourself,** honestly, do you really have to …? Okay, I'll shut up.

	Weekly	Fortnightly	Monthly	Quarterly	Annually
Beauty treatments					

APPEARANCE

LIFESTYLE
Have fun!

Wow, it costs quite a lot just to keep a human housed, fed, clothed and generally alive—am I right? It's also important to let you hair down, on occasion (which is, I must say, much easier when you don't cut it …).

Budgets that fail to account for spending on all the fun things in life will inevitably fail—they're just too restrictive. But if money is tight, this is also a category where you can definitely cut back on spending as you need.

Importantly, the 'Lifestyle' category includes all spending on eating out, fast food and takeaways—including those takeaway coffees! Any food you cook and eat at home goes in the 'Food' category—everything else goes here.

All alcohol, including what you consume at home, also goes here, along with an assortment of other traditional sins such as tobacco, drugs and sex services.

Holidays are the biggest lifestyle expense for many families. It's also important to plan financially for seasonal celebrations such as Christmas and birthdays.

The list of lifestyle sub-categories is long, but do have a read through them all. You never know, it may spark some ideas for incorporating a little more fun into both your budget and your life! It's amazing the array of activities humans get up to.

Eating out and takeaway

Include meals eaten out in restaurants, hotels and clubs; fast food, takeaway food and delivered; as well as takeaway coffees and school lunch money.

LIFESTYLE HACKS

My top 3 hacks for avoiding eating out and takeaway

☐ **Cook in bulk and freeze portions.** You'll never have an excuse not to grab something from the freezer to take to work for lunch. Note that you can also freeze sandwiches and let them thaw out during the morning.

☐ **Try keeping long-lasting food** such as tinned tuna, tinned beans, wraps and nuts at work so that you're never caught short.

☐ **Keep some emergency convenience meals in your freezer.** Yes, it might be cheaper to prepare all your own meals from scratch, but if this stops you ordering Uber Eats. It's a win.

	Weekly	Fortnightly	Monthly	Quarterly	Annually
Eating out and takeaway					

Alcohol

I once decided to give up alcohol for an entire year. I managed for eight months before deciding it was something that I can actually enjoy in moderation. I only drink socially these days, never alone. Turns out, after eight months off, you become quite a cheap drunk anyway. I definitely recommend experimenting with giving up the booze.

LIFESTYLE HACKS

My top hack for reducing alcohol costs

Try giving up alcohol for a period of time. Start with a week and see if you can stretch it out to a month. Alternatively, experiment with only drinking on weekends or when you're out of the house.

	Weekly	Fortnightly	Monthly	Quarterly	Annually
Alcohol					

Tobacco and drugs

Both legal and illegal … include here the cost of tobacco, cigarettes, cigars, e-cigarettes, vapes, narcotics and marijuana for both recreational and medicinal purposes.

	Weekly	Fortnightly	Monthly	Quarterly	Annually
Tobacco and drugs					

Holidays

Set yourself an annual sum that you would like to spend on holidays, both domestic and overseas. Budget for all costs, including travel, accommodation, travel insurance and entertainment. If you need it or want it while on your trip, set a budget for it here.

LIFESTYLE HACKS

My top 7 holiday costs hacks

☐ **Try to plan your holidays outside of school holidays and seasonal peak times** as the cost will usually be cheaper.

☐ **Plan your holidays well in advance** because you will often pay much less for flights and accommodation.

☐ **Opt for accommodation where you have the option to cook your own meals**, such as Airbnbs, home stays or serviced apartments.

- ☐ **Investigate domestic and international 'home swap' sites** where you can offer your own home as accommodation while you stay at someone else's place for free.
- ☐ **Share the expenses.** If you're going on group holidays, use an app such as KittySplit to divvy up expenses so you don't end up paying for all of Sandra's cocktails …
- ☐ **Save money on kennels** by forming a dog-sitting club with friends.
- ☐ **Become a pet-sitter for someone in a nice location.** Visit pet-sitting websites like Pet Cloud and Mad Paws to register.

	Weekly	Fortnightly	Monthly	Quarterly	Annually
Holidays					

Seasonal celebrations

These just keep getting bigger and bigger! They are such fun times of the year, but can really derail budgets. Include the cost here of all holiday decorations and food for Christmas, Halloween and Easter and for any other holidays, including Hanukkah, Eid, Diwali or similar. You might like to set a separate amount for each holiday you celebrate. Budget for gifts separately (see 'Gifts' later).

LIFESTYLE HACKS
My top celebration hack

Buy seasonal decorations and party wear on sale after the holiday and store them for the following year. You'll pay a fraction of the price!

	Weekly	Fortnightly	Monthly	Quarterly	Annually
Seasonal celebrations					

Parties and functions

The average Australian couple spends $36 000 on their wedding, according to the government's MoneySmart website. There's the venue, food, alcohol, music, photography, attire, rings and honeymoon to think about.

Of course, you don't get married every year (unless you're doing something quite wrong). But make sure you budget for the cost of attending other people's weddings, parties and events, as well as any parties and events you organise throughout the year.

LIFESTYLE HACKS
My top 6 wedding and party hacks

- [ ] **Don't spend your home deposit on a wedding.**
- [ ] **Ask for cash** via a wedding wishing well.
- [ ] **Have weddings on non-traditional days** such as a Friday.
- [ ] **Shop around and haggle** with suppliers.
- [ ] **Buy bulk decorations second hand,** then resell them when you're done!

☐ **Buy rings second hand.** Check auction houses and diamond wholesalers for second-hand jewellery. Gals, listen to Aunty Jess. Wedding rings sell for approximately one-third of the price you paid for them, so don't kid yourself you're making an investment. Just consider it, at least. And remember, when you do buy expensive jewellery, you also end up paying more to insure it. You can find second-hand diamonds through online diamond exchanges, antique jewellers and Facebook buy, swap and sell groups. Ask for a certificate of authenticity and buyer beware.

	Weekly	Fortnightly	Monthly	Quarterly	Annually
Parties and functions					

Gifts

This is whatever sum you wish to set aside to buy gifts throughout the year for family members and friends, including wrapping paper and cards. Think birthdays and Christmas, as well as any other occasions you celebrate, and don't forget Mother's Day, Father's Day and Valentine's Day.

LIFESTYLE HACKS
My top 4 hacks for gift giving

☐ **Talk to your family and friends about whether you wish to receive gifts or not.** Sometimes it's not necessary, particularly if loved ones know you are saving towards a goal.

(continued)

- [ ] **Give the gift of attention!** Promise a massage, a foot rub or a long walk together.

- [ ] **Agree to give and receive second-hand things:** if you shop in a charity store, you'll get extra warm and fuzzies from knowing you have helped others in need with your purchase.

- [ ] **Consider a 'Secret Santa'** so that you only need to buy one gift, rather than one for each member of the family.

	Weekly	Fortnightly	Monthly	Quarterly	Annually
Gifts					

Toys

If you have children, keeping them entertained can be a challenge. New toys are often bought and forgotten within a day. Which is not to say you shouldn't treat your little ones, but also consider these hacks.

LIFESTYLE HACKS

My top 5 hacks for saving on toys

- [ ] **Consider setting a 'budget' for your child to spend as they see fit.** This avoids arguments and introduces the idea of scarcity!

- [ ] **Seek out and accept hand-me-down toys** from friends, family and neighbours. There's a temptation as a new parent to buy everything new, but it's not necessary.

	Weekly	Fortnightly	Monthly	Quarterly	Annually
Toys					

Streaming services

Include here the cost of all Pay TV and streaming service subscriptions such as Netflix, Stan, Foxtel, Amazon Prime, Disney+, Hayu, Binge, Paramount+, Apple TV+, Kayo, Acorn TV, BritBox and MUBI.

LIFESTYLE

	Weekly	Fortnightly	Monthly	Quarterly	Annually
Streaming services					

Gaming and consoles

Include here the cost of all computer games and subscriptions and any physical consoles or other gaming equipment used purely for entertainment purposes.

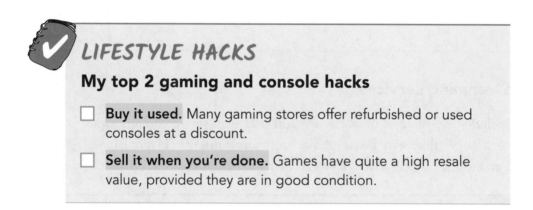

LIFESTYLE HACKS

My top 2 gaming and console hacks

☐ **Buy it used.** Many gaming stores offer refurbished or used consoles at a discount.

☐ **Sell it when you're done.** Games have quite a high resale value, provided they are in good condition.

	Weekly	Fortnightly	Monthly	Quarterly	Annually
Gaming and consoles					

LIFESTYLE

Music, audio and photographic

Include musical instruments, cameras, photo equipment and music downloads, purchases and streaming services such as Spotify.

LIFESTYLE HACKS

My top hack for enjoying free music

Many music streaming services offer free versions, provided you don't mind a few ads. Do you really need to pay?

	Weekly	Fortnightly	Monthly	Quarterly	Annually
Music, audio and photographic					

Live entertainment

Tally up all those nights at the theatre, concerts, cinema, ballet, opera, spectator sport admission fees, and dance and night club entry fees. Include the cost of any babysitting and dog-minding needed to attend.

LIFESTYLE HACKS

My top 4 live entertainment hacks

☐ **Ask what discounts may be available to you at the cinema,** including for motoring club members, unions and other concessions.

(continued)

LIFESTYLE

	Weekly	Fortnightly	Monthly	Quarterly	Annually
Live entertainment					

Attractions

Tickets and entry fees to national parks, zoos, theme parks, art galleries and museums.

✔ ## LIFESTYLE HACKS

My top hack for free entry passes

Investigate free museums, galleries and botanic gardens to visit in your area.

	Weekly	Fortnightly	Monthly	Quarterly	Annually
Attractions					

LIFESTYLE

Hobbies

The United Nations' list of human hobbies provides quite the technicoloured spectrum of potential human pursuits. Choose from the following outdoor hobbies: camping, sailing, kayaking, windsurfing, canoeing, sea diving, planes, gliders, hot-air balloons, campervans, caravans, trailers, horses, golf carts, billiard tables, ping-pong tables, quad-bikes, electric skateboards, electric kick scooters and 'self-balancing unicycles'.

If you prefer to stay indoors, there's art and craft hobbies. I'm also including under indoor hobbies dating apps, sex toys, and payments to sex workers and at strip clubs. They have to go somewhere and these are predominantly—although, by no means exclusively—indoor activities. Er hem.

✔ LIFESTYLE HACKS

My top hobby savings hack

Hobby equipment is a great thing to consider buying second hand as many people try a new hobby and don't stick at it. You might also soon find you're not so enthused, so try borrowing equipment from a friend or buying cheap before you over-commit!

	Weekly	Fortnightly	Monthly	Quarterly	Annually
Hobbies					

Gambling

This includes lottery tickets, casinos, gaming machines, bingo halls, scratch cards, sweepstakes and any other money spent on 'games of chance'.

✓ LIFESTYLE HACKS

My top 2 hacks for tackling a gambling habit

☐ **Remind yourself that the house always wins.** Gambling establishments can only survive if they receive more from gamblers in total than they pay out. If you do happen to win, quit while you're ahead.

☐ **Get help.** If gambling is a problem for you, call the Gambling Helpline on 1800 858 858. The National Debt Helpline (1800 007 007) can also help you if you've incurred debts. Under 25s can call the Gambler's Help Youthline on 1800 262 376 for tailored support.

	Weekly	Fortnightly	Monthly	Quarterly	Annually
Gambling					

Pet purchases

Consider any money you might want to pay for a puppy, kitten, bird, fish or other new pet. Consider also the set-up costs of collars, leashes, kennels, birdcages, fish tanks and cat litter trays. Once you bring your pet home, count all their other food and healthcare costs under their respective categories. They're family now.

LIFESTYLE HACKS
My top hack for pet purchases

Consider adopting a pet from the pound rather than buying a new puppy from a breeder. You will still incur some upfront costs, but they will be significantly less. Of course, it's hard to put a price on love.

	Weekly	Fortnightly	Monthly	Quarterly	Annually
Pet purchases					

•••

Well, that was fun! Nearly there now. Next we tackle our final category, which is 'Professional fees'.

LIFESTYLE

PROFESSIONAL FEES

Pay people to help you

I like to joke that this final category covers all my 'white collar dimes'. It's not exactly criminal, but we can end up forking out a lot over a lifetime to a host of professional service providers, particularly in the financial services sector.

This is the place to include your minimum repayments on any debts not already covered, including credit cards and personal loans.

Then there's a host of other payments to professionals such as lawyers, accountants and financial advisors.

I also include in this category a couple of other sundry expenses, including payments to children for pocket money, payments to exes for child support, payments to unions to represent you as a worker and payments to charities to do good work in the world on your behalf. Essentially, these are all payments to third parties, if not exactly white-collared ones, and they need to go somewhere.

Also include the cost of policies held for life and income protection insurance, if you hold them outside of your superannuation. Do not include policy premiums deducted out of super. Don't forget about those, but don't include them here as they don't reduce today's disposable income (they just eat into your future nest egg).

Credit cards

Credit card interest is an expense you really should avoid by paying off your credit card in full each month. But since that's not always possible, enter your required minimum payments each month below. You can and should make additional payments to try to clear your debts, but these can be made out of your calculated budget surplus. We're just interested here in the costs you can't avoid each month.

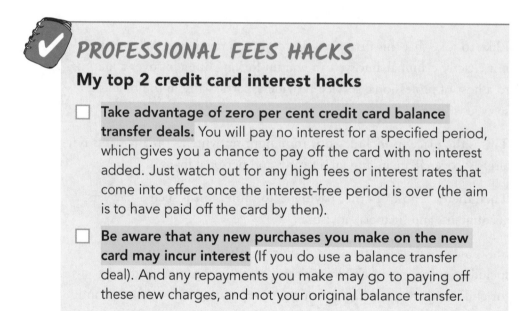

PROFESSIONAL FEES HACKS

My top 2 credit card interest hacks

☐ **Take advantage of zero per cent credit card balance transfer deals.** You will pay no interest for a specified period, which gives you a chance to pay off the card with no interest added. Just watch out for any high fees or interest rates that come into effect once the interest-free period is over (the aim is to have paid off the card by then).

☐ **Be aware that any new purchases you make on the new card may incur interest** (If you do use a balance transfer deal). And any repayments you make may go to paying off these new charges, and not your original balance transfer.

	Weekly	Fortnightly	Monthly	Quarterly	Annually
Credit cards					

Other loans

This is the place to pop repayments you're obliged to make on any other loans, including Buy Now Pay Later payments and money borrowed from family or friends.

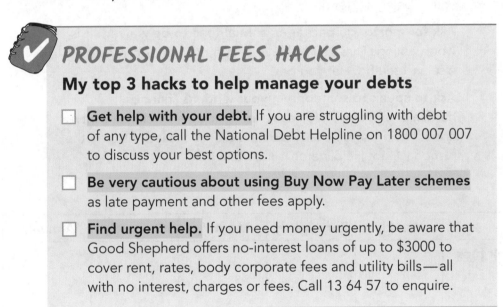

PROFESSIONAL FEES HACKS

My top 3 hacks to help manage your debts

☐ **Get help with your debt.** If you are struggling with debt of any type, call the National Debt Helpline on 1800 007 007 to discuss your best options.

☐ **Be very cautious about using Buy Now Pay Later schemes** as late payment and other fees apply.

☐ **Find urgent help.** If you need money urgently, be aware that Good Shepherd offers no-interest loans of up to $3000 to cover rent, rates, body corporate fees and utility bills—all with no interest, charges or fees. Call 13 64 57 to enquire.

	Weekly	Fortnightly	Monthly	Quarterly	Annually
Other loans					

PROFESSIONAL FEES

Bank fees

Bank fees have fallen dramatically, but there are still ways to avoid being stung.

	Weekly	Fortnightly	Monthly	Quarterly	Annually
Bank fees					

Life / trauma / TPD insurance

Many people are unaware they have insurance cover for major life illnesses or Total and Permanent Disability (TPD) death, through their superannuation accounts.

	Weekly	Fortnightly	Monthly	Quarterly	Annually
Life / trauma / TPD insurance					

Income protection insurance

Income protection insurance is designed to pay out in the event you are unable to work. There are a dizzying array of options and types and it can be worth seeking advice on which will best suit your needs.

PROFESSIONAL FEES

	Weekly	Fortnightly	Monthly	Quarterly	Annually
Income protection insurance					

Financial advisor fees

Financial advice has become much more expensive in recent years, partly because the government has acted to clean up standards in the industry. Seeking advice can often come with a minimum price tag of $3000.

✔ PROFESSIONAL FEES HACKS

My top 6 hacks for reducing financial advice costs

☐ **Ask for a free initial consult** with any advisor to see if they are able to help you with your needs.

☐ **Create a concise list of the main questions you want answered** so that you are prepared.

☐ **Speak to several financial advisors** and go with the one who seems most trustworthy.

☐ **Ask family and friends for recommendations** as a starting point.

☐ **Make sure any advisor you see is registered with Australian Securities and Investment Commission (ASIC),** which maintains a register of advisors on its website.

☐ **Check if your employer's Employee Assistance Program includes access to free financial counseling.**

	Weekly	Fortnightly	Monthly	Quarterly	Annually
Financial advisor fees					

Accountant / tax agent fees

If you have investment properties or complex tax affairs, it can pay to seek professional support to maximise your potential deductions.

✔ PROFESSIONAL FEES HACKS

My top accounting hack

Don't forget to claim the cost of managing your tax affairs as a deduction come tax time!

	Weekly	Fortnightly	Monthly	Quarterly	Annually
Accountant / tax agent fees					

Legal fees

Sometimes in life, it is unavoidable to need to seek the support of a trained lawyer.

PROFESSIONAL FEES HACKS

My top 2 hacks for reducing legal fees

- [ ] **Be clear about your financial means to pay**, and discuss a ballpark estimate of how much advice will cost.

- [ ] **Research legal aid centres in your state** to see if you can access free support.

	Weekly	Fortnightly	Monthly	Quarterly	Annually
Legal fees					

Funeral expenses

Include here the cost of any funeral plans or money you wish to set aside regularly for funeral expenses.

PROFESSIONAL FEES HACKS

My top hack for paying funeral costs

Beware of expensive funeral insurance policies for which you can end up paying more in premiums than the cost of a funeral. Investigate 'funeral bonds' instead or just start setting aside regular savings into a savings account to cover expenses.

	Weekly	Fortnightly	Monthly	Quarterly	Annually
Funeral expenses					

Union / professional association fees

If you pay ongoing fees to be a member of a union or a professional association, don't forget to account for them here.

PROFESSIONAL FEES HACKS

My top hack

Don't forget to tax deduct these costs.

	Weekly	Fortnightly	Monthly	Quarterly	Annually
Union / professional association fees					

PROFESSIONAL FEES

Child support

If you pay money to a parent of your child to cover their costs, this is the place to pop those payments. Okay, so it might seem a bit strange to some to classify this as a 'professional fee', but it needs to go somewhere!

	Weekly	Fortnightly	Monthly	Quarterly	Annually
Child support					

Pocket money

Write any allowances for children here. Hopefully they'll act in a courteous and professional manner in return, but I can't guarantee it. This is also where I budget for tooth-fairy money!

	Weekly	Fortnightly	Monthly	Quarterly	Annually
Pocket money					

Charity donations

Regular or one-off donations are a key part of many people's budgets. I've put them here because, in one sense, you're paying professional helpers to do good on your behalf in the world.

PROFESSIONAL FEES HACKS

My top donations hack

If your donation is to a registered charity, be sure to claim your deductions at tax time! You can check your charity's tax status via the register on the Australian Charities and Not-for-profits Commission website.

	Weekly	Fortnightly	Monthly	Quarterly	Annually
Charity donations					

• • •

Phew! You're all done! Congratulations on making it through all 10 of my budget categories. I hope it's given you an opportunity to think about some of the costs many people forget. If you've skimmed over some, don't worry. You can always come back to them.

In the next chapter, we're going to have some fun. This is where we put all the puzzle pieces from this chapter together to create your personal annual budget.

7

Create your very own budget

Annual budgets are an important ritual in democracies. Once a year, a treasurer or finance minister prepares an annual budget to present to the country's citizens.

The purpose of such budgets is to keep taxpayers informed of how their hard-earned dollars are being spent. They are snapshots in time: a government's best estimates of its future income, expenditure and the resulting annual surplus or deficit of funds.

As fancy as they look, these annual budgets are just guesstimates, of course, usually presented a couple of months in advance of the financial year to which they apply. Final budget outcomes can end up looking *very* different from what is forecast—for example, economic downturns can deliver an unanticipated hit to revenues and spending demands may rise.

But, as imperfect as they may ultimately turn out to be, budgets are a necessary feature of a well-run government. And, I would argue, a well-run household! Yes, things may deviate from the intended path—household incomes can shrink and bills may blow out—but it's important to at least try to think ahead.

We've just conducted a huge fishing expedition in chapter 6, flinging a net far and wide to capture every possible expense that could come up in your budget. Now it's time to haul it in and study your findings.

To make a budget, you need to be able to answer three questions:

1. How much money is coming in?
2. How much money is going out?
3. What's left over, if anything?

The answers to these questions combined represent your budget. Remember I said a budget could be as simple as writing on a piece of paper? In this chapter, I'll run you through each of these three questions in turn, giving you space, if you choose, to record your answers in this book. In a physical sense, this will make the book your budget. I'm honoured to be on the cover!

Alternatively, or in addition, you can download Excel and PDF versions of my Annual Budget worksheet from my website, jessicairvine.com.au, to assist you in calculating your numbers. They're completely free and you can download as many copies as you like (in case you stuff up before you get it right!). A little bit of trial and error is entirely normal and to be expected. Or, if you're using the Excel version, you can type in your numbers right there on the screen and amend them as often as you like.

Okay, let's make you a budget …

Money in: what is your income?

Firstly, it's important to be clear on what income figure you should use in your budget.

The income you want to focus on here is your 'disposable' income—that is, the income you actually have 'at your disposal'. This is the amount that directly hits your bank account after your employer has withheld both tax and compulsory superannuation contributions.

This is also sometimes known as your 'after-tax' or 'take-home' pay. But I like saying 'disposable' because it reminds me of a fancy English butler going to work for you: 'Good morning, Sir. What would you like to buy today? I am entirely at your disposal'. *bows courteously*

One of my mantras in life is to try not to worry about things I can't control.

Ain't nothing surer than death and taxes, of course, so I ignore taxes in my budget. There are lots of ways to try to reduce your taxes owing when it comes to submitting your tax return, but throughout the year you generally can't control what portion your employer withholds for tax purposes. So ignore it and only focus on your regular after-tax income here.

Similarly with super. Yes, your super money is 'real' money too, but there's not a lot you can do about the government mandating that 10 per cent of your salary be whisked away into your retirement account. That transaction is locked in—you can't control it. So we won't track it here either.

Note that it is also possible to instruct your employer to make additional voluntary contributions to your super on your behalf from your pre-tax income, so you never actually see it in your bank account. I do this and I also exclude it from my income for budgeting purposes. Here's how it works.

Should you make voluntary contributions to your super?

Australian workers are able to contribute a total of $27 500 (currently) into their super accounts each year and pay only the low tax rate of 15 cents in the dollar on that money (provided they earn less than $250 000).

If your marginal tax rate is higher than 15 per cent, this can be a great little money saver—provided you don't mind not seeing your money again until you're over 60.

This $27 500 amount includes any compulsory employer contributions made on your behalf. For example, if you earn $80 000 and your employer contributes at the 10 per cent rate, your compulsory superannuation amount would be $8000. That still leaves you with space to contribute up to $19 500 a year of your own money ($27 500 minus $8000).

You can make voluntary contributions in two ways.

The first is to simply make an 'after-tax' transfer into your retirement account from your savings. This money has already had tax applied at the higher rate, so you are eligible to claim any contributions this way as a tax deduction come tax time. You might get a tidy little tax return that year! (Just remember to speak to your super fund first, as there is some paperwork titled a 'Notice of intent to claim' that needs to be filled in and sent to the tax office for you to be able to claim this deduction.)

Alternatively, you can choose to 'salary sacrifice' extra money into super. As the name implies, this involves 'sacrificing' by not receiving upfront some of your salary but instead having it transferred by your employer into your super account. Crucially, your employer will not have to withhold income tax against this part of your income. It goes straight to super where the fund withholds 15 per cent and sends it to the tax office instead. You're still taxed, but at a lower rate (provided your marginal rate is higher than 15 cents).

For lower income earners, there are other incentives available to help you boost your super. Employees earning less than $37 000 a year may be eligible to receive the Low Income Super Tax Offset (LISTO) of up to $500 a year if they make voluntary contributions to their super. Couples where one partner earns less than $40,000 (including super) may also benefit from a tax offset of up to $540 available where the higher income partner makes a 'spouse contribution' to the low income partner's super fund. It is always worth a phone call to your super fund to see what government incentives may be on offer to you to help turbo-charge your retirement savings.

Something worth considering.

So here is my first question for you: what is your annual disposable income?

This is the time to get out your latest payslip and calculate exactly how much hits your bank account. Also get out your partner's payslips if you're budgeting as a couple or a household. Go on, I'll wait ...

Of course, this question is much easier for regular salary earners. But what about casual workers or people whose income fluctuates for various reasons? Don't worry, I see you.

You have a couple of options. You can look back over the past year and simply assume that as your annual income this year. Or, can use your judgement to guess how much you expect to receive this year. Or, you can create your budget based off the minimum income you know you are sure to receive this year.

For everyone, I have provided a table below for you to list all your sources of income, salary and otherwise. Non-salary income can include government benefits, child support, bonuses or overtime, small business or side-hustle income, cash gifts or income from investments such as dividends or net returns from investment properties (remember, I said in chapter 6 in my 'Note to owners of multiple properties' to keep a separate tally of that).

Remember to only include the disposable portion of this income—that is, the amount you get to keep. Income from small businesses, investments and some side hustles are taxable. If this applies to you, you'll need to remember that a proportion of what you receive will need to go to the tax office, if tax hasn't already been withheld. So only include in your budget an estimate of what you expect to keep after tax. If, say, your marginal tax rate is 32.5 cents, deduct that amount from every dollar of taxable income.

Okay, over to you …

Estimated annual income

Income source	Amount
Salary or wage	$.
Overtime	$.
Bonus	$.
Small business income	$.
Side-hustle income	$.
Government benefits and payments	$.
Child support	$.
Investment property net income	$.
Dividends from shares	$.
Other income	$.
TOTAL INCOME	$.

Yay, you've performed the first of the three steps to creating your budget!

Now that you have an estimate for your income, it's worth having a think about ways to increase it, in addition to all my killer suggestions for getting a pay rise in chapter 4. I'm all about you being proactive and generating some extra side-hustle income in the ways below, but do make sure you're being paid correctly in your day job first.

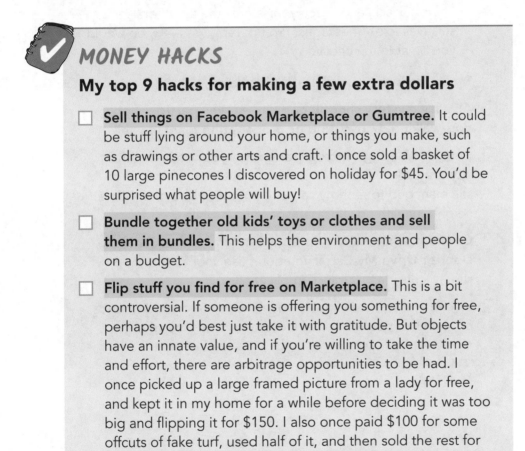

MONEY HACKS

My top 9 hacks for making a few extra dollars

☐ **Sell things on Facebook Marketplace or Gumtree.** It could be stuff lying around your home, or things you make, such as drawings or other arts and craft. I once sold a basket of 10 large pinecones I discovered on holiday for $45. You'd be surprised what people will buy!

☐ **Bundle together old kids' toys or clothes and sell them in bundles.** This helps the environment and people on a budget.

☐ **Flip stuff you find for free on Marketplace.** This is a bit controversial. If someone is offering you something for free, perhaps you'd best just take it with gratitude. But objects have an innate value, and if you're willing to take the time and effort, there are arbitrage opportunities to be had. I once picked up a large framed picture from a lady for free, and kept it in my home for a while before deciding it was too big and flipping it for $150. I also once paid $100 for some offcuts of fake turf, used half of it, and then sold the rest for $100. I've spent more time on Facebook Marketplace than anyone needs to know about.

(continued)

- ☐ **When selling on Marketplace, make sure you:**
  - *take lots of photos*, including of any damage
  - *write a detailed description*: use lots of key search words—don't just write 'bookcase', write 'book', 'case', 'shelf', 'white', 'coastal', 'Hamptons' (in fact, write 'Hamptons' for anything and people will buy it).

    Then sit back, and brace yourself for the storm of 'Is this still available?' messages. Pro tip: reply 'Yes—when would you be able to collect?'

- ☐ **Try advertising your skills on Airtasker.**
- ☐ **Also try mystery shopping, online survey participation, dog-walking, babysitting or propagating plants to sell.**
- ☐ **Consider leasing out your car spot if you are in an inner city area.** I live about 10 kilometres out from the city and still managed to rent my car spot out for $180 a month to a neighbour with no allocated space for a while.
- ☐ **Consider schemes to rent out your car, such as Car Next Door or Drive My Car**, if you don't use your car much. Be sure to consider insurance implications.
- ☐ **Invest!** This will earn you 'passive' income such as dividends on shares or possibly rental income from an investment property. We'll get to this.

Money out: what are your expenses?

Now comes the really fun part. We're going to take all the amounts you entered into the tables in chapter 6 and combine them for a complete picture of your annual spending.

To help get you started, and to prove that I practice what I preach, I'm going to share with you a snapshot of my own household spending.

Remember when I wrote that I once tracked every dollar I spent for an entire year? Well, on the next page you will find an a snapshot of my actual annual spending for 2020–21, sorted into my 10 budget categories. (I share more of how I track my spending in part III.)

Try not to get too hung up on my figures. Everyone's household is different. These figures are for a high-income, single-parent household living in Sydney during a year of COVID-19 and associated lockdowns. What a year it was!

But I do think it's useful to have someone to compare notes with. And if you don't have anyone else in your life to compare your figures to, well, you do now. I'll show you mine if you promise to also calculate yours, okay …?

MY ANNUAL BUDGET

YEAR <u>2020-21</u>

HOUSING	Annual cost
HOUSING	$34 244.28

HOUSEHOLD	Annual cost
Furniture	$ 659.40
Décor	$ 169.61
Appliances	$.
Home maintenance and repairs	$.
Cleaning	$ 224.03
Hygiene	$ 191.50
Garden	$.
Strata fees	$ 6818.12
Home insurance	$ 260.66
Council rates	$ 1155.56
Household services	$.
TOTAL	$9478.88

UTILITIES	Annual cost
Electricity	$ 1184.44
Gas	$.
Water and sewerage	$ 584.44
Internet	$ 814.83
Phone	$.
Postal services	$.
TOTAL	$2583.71

TRANSPORT	Annual cost
Vehicle purchase	$.
Vehicle loan payments	$.

	Annual cost
Vehicle registration	$ 377.00
Drivers licence	$.
Vehicle insurance	$ 908.46
Vehicle servicing and repairs	$ 2438.23
Vehicle parts and accessories	$ 580.00
Roadside assist	$ 128.00
Driving lessons	$.
Fuel	$ 1209.72
Tolls	$ 140.03
Parking	$ 573.42
Public transport	$ 254.73
Vehicle hire, taxis and ride shares	$ 27.74
TOTAL	$6637.33

FOOD	Annual cost
FOOD	$5318.33

HEALTH	Annual cost
Health insurance	$ 809.13
Pet insurance and veterinary costs	$.
Doctors and specialists	$ 1245.27
Dental	$ 312.00
Optical	$.
Hospital and ambulance	$.
Medicines	$ 420.34
Medical equipment	$.
Sport and fitness	$ 3961.38
TOTAL	$6748.12

Remember not to get toooo hung up on my exact numbers (although isn't it fascinating to see what other people spend?!) Every household is unique. I just want to show you it's possible to create a complete snapshot of your spending.

EDUCATION	Annual cost
Books, newspapers and magazines	$ 457 . 06
Stationery	$ 338 . 62
Home computer equipment	$ 78 . 00
Childcare	$ 1692 . 38
School	$ 10031 . 70
Higher education	$.
TOTAL	$ 12597 . 76

APPEARANCE	Annual cost
Clothes and shoes	$ 303 . 38
Accessories	$.
Hairdressing	$ 85 . 50
Beauty products	$ 17 . 99
Beauty treatments	$.
TOTAL	$ 405 . 87

LIFESTYLE	Annual cost
Eating out and takeaway	$ 1393 . 76
Alcohol	$ 157 . 21
Tobacco and drugs	$.
Holidays	$ 4579 . 03
Seasonal celebrations	$ 14 . 95
Parties and functions	$.
Gifts	$ 859 . 39
Toys	$ 794 . 46
Streaming services	$ 195 . 82
Gaming and consoles	$ 149 . 02
Music, audio and photographic	$ 6 . 57
Live entertainment	$ 230 . 00
Attractions	$ 68 . 90

Hobbies	$ 570 . 66
Gambling	$.
Pet purchases	$.
TOTAL	$ 9019 . 77

PROFESSIONAL FEES	Annual cost
Credit cards	$.
Other loans	$.
Bank fees	$ 493 . 00
Life / trauma / TPD insurance	$.
Income protection insurance	$.
Financial advisor fees	$.
Accountant / tax agent fees	$.
Legal fees	$ 153 . 99
Funeral expenses	$.
Union / professional association fees	$ 688 . 80
Child support	$.
Pocket money	$ 10 . 00
Charity donations	$.
TOTAL	$ 1345 . 79

TOTAL INCOME	$.

TOTAL EXPENSES	$ 88 379 . 84

SURPLUS	$.

Also, remember these figures are my ACTUAL spending for one year. Your annual budget estimates won't be as precise, and that's absolutely as it should be.

Ok, it's time to make your annual budget!

Hopefully you'll have been following my advice at the start of chapter 6 to tally an annual figure for all your sub-categories as you work through them. That way, it's now just a matter of going back to your estimates and transferring them into the table on the next page.

Alternatively, if you've downloaded and used the Excel version of my Annual Budget worksheet, the spreadsheet will tabulate this for you.

Don't worry if you mess up writing in the Annual Budget worksheet here in this book—you can download the exact same worksheet in PDF form from my website. Download and print out as many copies as you like!

Bonus points if you highlight your entries using the colours you assigned to your categories. 😊

MY ANNUAL BUDGET

YEAR

	Annual cost
HOUSING	$.

HOUSEHOLD	Annual cost
Furniture	$.
Décor	$.
Appliances	$.
Home maintenance and repairs	$.
Cleaning	$.
Hygiene	$.
Garden	$.
Strata fees	$.
Home insurance	$.
Council rates	$.
Household services	$.
TOTAL	$.

UTILITIES	Annual cost
Electricity	$.
Gas	$.
Water and sewerage	$.
Internet	$.
Phone	$.
Postal services	$.
TOTAL	$.

TRANSPORT	Annual cost
Vehicle purchase	$.
Vehicle loan payments	$.

	Annual cost
Vehicle registration	$.
Drivers licence	$.
Vehicle insurance	$.
Vehicle servicing and repairs	$.
Vehicle parts and accessories	$.
Roadside assist	$.
Driving lessons	$.
Fuel	$.
Tolls	$.
Parking	$.
Public transport	$.
Vehicle hire, taxis and ride shares	$.
TOTAL	$.

	Annual cost
FOOD	$.

HEALTH	Annual cost
Health insurance	$.
Pet insurance and veterinary costs	$.
Doctors and specialists	$.
Dental	$.
Optical	$.
Hospital and ambulance	$.
Medicines	$.
Medical equipment	$.
Sport and fitness	$.
TOTAL	$.

EDUCATION

EDUCATION	Annual cost
Books, newspapers and magazines	$.
Stationery	$.
Home computer equipment	$.
Childcare	$.
School	$.
Higher education	$.
TOTAL	$.

APPEARANCE

APPEARANCE	Annual cost
Clothes and shoes	$.
Accessories	$.
Hairdressing	$.
Beauty products	$.
Beauty treatments	$.
TOTAL	$.

LIFESTYLE

LIFESTYLE	Annual cost
Eating out and takeaway	$.
Alcohol	$.
Tobacco and drugs	$.
Holidays	$.
Seasonal celebrations	$.
Parties and functions	$.
Gifts	$.
Toys	$.
Streaming services	$.
Gaming and consoles	$.
Music, audio and photographic	$.
Live entertainment	$.
Attractions	$.

	Annual cost
Hobbies	$.
Gambling	$.
Pet purchases	$.
TOTAL	$.

PROFESSIONAL FEES

PROFESSIONAL FEES	Annual cost
Credit cards	$.
Other loans	$.
Bank fees	$.
Life / trauma / TPD insurance	$.
Income protection insurance	$.
Financial advisor fees	$.
Accountant / tax agent fees	$.
Legal fees	$.
Funeral expenses	$.
Union / professional association fees	$.
Child support	$.
Pocket money	$.
Charity donations	$.
TOTAL	$.

TOTAL INCOME	$.

TOTAL EXPENSES	$.

SURPLUS	$.

Gosh, it all adds up, doesn't it?

Now, I hope you can see how useful having this information is.

First, it enables you to calculate the appropriate size of your emergency fund. As you can see, my annual spend was $88 380. Divide that by 12 and you'll find that my average monthly spend was $7365.

If I wanted to have an emergency fund containing six months of my current living expenses, I would need to set aside $44 190. If I wanted a three-month fund, I'd be aiming for $22 095.

Alternatively, I might decide that in the event of an emergency, I could probably live a more modest lifestyle. If I knocked out my 'Lifestyle' category expenses ($9020) and my substantial gym membership fees ($3961 a year), my annual expenses would fall to $75 399, so $6283 a month. That'd mean a six-month emergency fund of $37 700 or a three-month fund of $18 850.

Currently, my emergency fund is sitting at $36 000 (it's in my mortgage offset account). This is the number that lets me sleep at night. Yours might be different.

Having this information at your fingertips also helps you to plan for retirement. My goal is to pay off my mortgage before I retire. That will knock about $34 000 a year off my living expenses. I also don't expect to have as many costs related to caring for my son, including the $10 032 I currently pay each year in school fees and other school costs. Knocking out these two expenses alone, with no other changes to my current lifestyle, reduces my annual living costs to $44 104.

Clearly that's still above what the full single-person age pension rate of $25 155 would provide. But it's okay — at the time of writing, I already have about $345 000 socked away in super.

When I punch that super balance into the government's online MoneySmart Retirement Planner (Google it and have a play!), it reckons I'm on course to draw an annual income in retirement of about $52 000 (if I keep making my contributions at the current rate and retire aged 60).

That sounds pretty manageable to me. If I push out my retirement until I'm 65, I should be able to expect an income of about $69 000 a year. Knowing these figures gives me such peace of mind.

But enough about me. Let's talk about you!

What are your current estimated annual living expenses? How big an emergency fund would that equate to for three or six months? What do you think could be a reasonable estimate of your household's annual living expenses in retirement?

Write some of your key figures in the spaces below:

Key annual expenses scenarios	Amount
Total annual living expenses	$.
Modest lifestyle annual living expenses:	$.
Goal emergency fund (modest living expenses figure multiplied by desired number of months)	$.
Anticipated retirement annual living expenses:	$.

Feel free to download a few copies of either the Excel or PDF versions of my Annual Budget worksheet and have a play with putting together some different types of budgets: one for lean times such as saving for a home deposit, one for a lean retirement, or one for a 'dream' retirement.

For any season of your life, you can play with your numbers to make them fit. Money might not grow on trees, but my free printable resources quite literally do (paper is made of trees — geddit?). So have a play!

Okay, time to move on.

It's time for the grand finale of your budget!

Drum roll please …

What's left? Are you in surplus or deficit?

Whip out your calculators again, folks. It's time for the punchline. When you subtract your annual expenses from your annual income, are you in surplus?

Write your numbers on your Annual Budget worksheet and below, if you wish …

My budget bottom line	Amount
Total income	$.
Total expenses	$.
Surplus/deficit	$.

If you're in deficit, please don't despair. There are so many ways you can explore to either boost your income or cut your expenses. I've provided you with more than 300 hacks in this book, so cast your eye back and see which ones you want to try. Write a list of ideas you want to try. Then get cracking! How good will it feel when you eke yourself out a surplus for the first time?

If you are in surplus, well done! Now you get to decide how you want to use this money to either pay off debts, build your emergency fund or invest, either directly or through contributions to your super. You'll find more information on your options for deploying your surplus in chapter 10.

If you were thinking about borrowing, either to invest or for home ownership, that's great; if you have a surplus, you have room in your budget to consider this. Remember that when you go to the bank, you don't have to give them your 'Shiraz and Wagyu' budget—just your 'minced beef and water' estimates (go back to the 'Housing' section of chapter 6 if you need a refresher on that).

But before you go running off and making major decisions based on your annual budget, I want you to pause and breathe for a moment.

Because here's the thing about budgets: they're not just a set-and-forget affair. Yes, you have achieved an extraordinary thing in creating an annual budget for yourself to estimate your income, expenses and resulting surplus or deficit. But it will likely need refining, particularly if this is the first time you've attempted to estimate your expenses and income.

And keep in mind that a year is a very long time: unexpected things could take place that reduce your income or up your expenses. You don't want to go deploying your surplus just yet—particularly into investments you can't easily withdraw from—until you're reasonably confident your estimates hold water.

To be confident of this, you're going to need to pay some closer attention—if only for a period of time—to where your money is really going and whether that lines up with your expectations. Which is why I have devoted the final part of my book—part III—to showing you the daily and monthly system I have created to maintain and look after my budget.

It's a system that gives me not only the peace of mind to know I'm covered for all the big expenses in my life, but also the confidence to regularly invest my surplus funds into the share market at the end of each month. Surely you'd like to know a little bit more about that?

PART III

How to maintain your budget

Now, promise me you're not going to be *that* guy. You know the one I mean: the one who waltzes into town, all big talk and promises, dazzles you with his impressive spreadsheet, and then he's gone first thing in the morning and you never hear from him again …

We're not ghosting our budgets, okay? 👻

You have just made a significant effort to create an annual budget to put you on the path to financial freedom. (Well done, by the way. I think you're amazing!) Know that doing that exercise alone puts you miles ahead of most people when it comes to understanding your money.

But if you really want your budget to keep working for you, you're going to need to keep showing it some love, okay? You're going to need a system—a set of habits—to nurture your money on a regular, ongoing basis. Well, aren't you lucky: I'm about to show you one I designed earlier!

I've been working on perfecting my regular budgeting routine since early 2020. You might have seen it on Instagram. It now involves three key components: tracking my spending, creating 'future funds' to smooth out lumpy expenses and filling out a Monthly Budget worksheet at the end of each month to see where my money went. I'm about to walk you through each in turn.

In chapter 8, I'll introduce you to my Spending Tracker, which I use to track all my expenses (yep, every single one!). I'll explain the benefits of committing to doing this for at least one month and why I prefer doing it by hand.

In chapter 9, I will show you how to set up your own 'future funds' using my Future Fund worksheets. Also known as 'sinking funds', these are a way of regularly setting money aside to avoid the bill shock of larger and less frequent expenses when they inevitably arrive.

Then, in chapter 10 I'll show you how to fill out my Monthly Budget worksheet. Remember, I regard a 'budget' as any statement that tallies your income, spending and resulting surplus or deficit over a period of time.

Now, I know you've just made an annual budget based on estimates of your expenditure (yay!), but I'm going to suggest you use my monthly budget worksheet to track your *actual* budget outcomes. This will enable you, over time, to compare how your actual spending compares to your estimates. It also enables you to see and invest any surplus money you have on a regular, monthly basis, rather than waiting until the end of the year, by which time you might have missed out on the wonders of compounding returns.

These chapters work together to outline the complete system I use personally to monitor my money each month. I keep printed versions of all the worksheets mentioned in a simple binder, which I have named *Jess' amazing folder of budgeting goodness* (that's literally written on the front). It's one of my most prized possessions. If you'd like to see what it looks like and how to create it, check out page 242 in chapter 10.

Remember, all the resources you'll need to work through part III are available to download for free from my website, jessicairvine.com.au.

Importantly, these worksheets are there to assist, not hinder you. If you would prefer to create your own routine for monitoring and reviewing your money, I fully support that. Take what you need from this book! If you have another system in place to keep checking in with your money, staying in surplus and investing, I am proud of you. Look at you go!

However, if you need a place to start, this is it.

This process brings me so much joy. I can't wait to share it with you.

8

Track
your spending

You may have noticed by now that my budgeting system is not one which encourages you to set arbitrary spending limits in advance and insists you keep to them.

This runs counter to a lot of common advice, being that you should set limits for spending, or targets for saving, and stick to them.

These limits are supposed to engender discipline and motivate you to save. But I think it often turns people off because they think that budgeting is restrictive and it may stop them from starting. People often have no idea what are realistic limits to set, so they find their budget too restrictive and just ditch it.

I think there is value in starting by simply observing your spending patterns first and then tweaking. Simply coming up with a snapshot of how much you spend in a month, versus how much you earn, can be an eye opener and enough motivation to want to pay closer attention.

For me, it's also about cultivating a sense of trust in myself that I have the power to say 'yes' to pleasant spending opportunities but also 'no' to mindless spending.

Simply committing to track my spending throughout each month, as I have, and then to calculate the surplus left over at the end of each month, sets up a real contest in my mind for every dollar I consider spending. Do I really want to spend $30 ordering Uber Eats? Or do I want to boost my end-of-month surplus by $30 by cooking the food I have in the fridge?

It gamifies it for me: I really look forward to the end of the month when I get to see how I did! More on this in Chapter 10!

Economists never want you following arbitrary rules and forcing yourself to stick to them. Economists advise you to 'think at the margin', which means constantly weighing the costs and benefits of each decision that you make.

The trick is that if you focus on the small details, and make lots of good spending decisions in a row—only buying things that truly bring you joy—all those small decisions start to add up, in the long run, to one happy life.

And you don't have to plan too far ahead.

You just look after the pennies and the pounds take care of themselves. Or, as my own personal money mantra says: 'dignity in every dollar'.

Of course, you can set mini goals for yourself, like trying to keep your monthly food budget to a certain amount. But just don't go beating yourself up if you go over your budget, okay? That won't help anyone.

All I want you to do is ask yourself, for every purchase that you make: 'Do the benefits of this purchase outweigh the costs?' And not just in dollar terms. But in terms of the time you had to give up to earn that money and the opportunities you will lose to do other necessary or pleasurable things in the future because you bought this item today.

I just want you to really stop and think about how you are spending your money. And the only way to do that, is by thoroughly observing yourself and where your money goes.

That's where my Spending Tracker worksheet comes in.

I manually record every dollar I spend, by hand and on a paper Spending Tracker I created that looks like this.

MY SPENDING TRACKER

MONTH __JANUARY__   YEAR _____

Date	Payment method	Expense	Category	Amount	Direct debt	Future Fund drawdown	Variable spending	Essential? Y/N	Entered?
3	offset	Bunnings sausage	LIFESTYLE	$ 2.50			×	N	○
4	"	Uber Eats	LIFESTYLE	$ 36.75			×	N	○
4	"	brunch with friend	LIFESTYLE	$ 18.00			×	N	○
5	"	beer @ pub	LIFESTYLE	$ 6.89			×	N	○
5	"	dinner @ pub	LIFESTYLE	$ 18.23			×	N	○
7	"	food @ Woolies	FOOD	$ 7.60			×	Y	○
7	"	food @ Aldi	FOOD	$ 261.42			×	Y	○
7	"	laundry liquid @ Aldi	HOUSEHOLD	$ 7.99			×	Y	○
7	"	sheet set @ Aldi	HOUSEHOLD	$ 34.99			×	N	○
7	"	book @ Aldi	EDUCATION	$ 9.99			×	N	○
10	"	psychologist ($210 – $129.55)	HEALTH	$ 80.45			×	Y	○
10	"	roadside assist	TRANSPORT	$ 132.00		×		Y	○
11	"	strata fees	HOUSEHOLD	$ 1988.63		×		Y	○
12	"	sushi train	LIFESTYLE	$ 37.78			×	N	○
14	"	internet	UTILITIES	$ 59.95	×			Y	○
15	"	new sunnies	APPEARANCE	$ 19.95			×	Y	○
15	"	Netflix	LIFESTYLE	$ 10.99	×			N	○
15	"	petrol	TRANSPORT	$ 84.68			×	Y	○
16	"	yoga class	HEALTH	$ 26.50			×	N	○
16	"	mortgage min. repay	HOUSING	$ 2599.00	×			Y	○
17	"	coffees x2	LIFESTYLE	$ 8.13			×	N	○
17	"	food @ Aldi	FOOD	$ 82.32			×	Y	○
17	"	textas + art book	EDUCATION	$ 4.98			×	N	○
17	"	paracetamol @ Aldi	HEALTH	$ .75			×	Y	○

Isn't it pretty?! See how all my expenses are highlighted with the colour I assigned to that category? And don't worry, I'm about to walk you through what all the other columns mean right now ☺ Also, how good are Bunnings sausages ... ?

If you turn forward one page, you can find a blank copy of my Spending Tracker in this book.

You can download and print as many copies of this tracker as you like — for free — from my website, jessicairvine.com.au.

The good news is you can start tracking your spending absolutely any time you like. Why not today?

How to use the Spending Tracker

The Spending Tracker is very straightforward to use. All you have to do is record every expense you incur for at least one month. I suggest doing this for 12 consecutive months so that you build a complete snapshot of one entire year's worth of expenses. But even if you do it for one month, you will see some benefits in terms of becoming more mindful of how you're spending your money.

Keep receipts or records of all your expenses and, every few days, update your Spending Tracker.

I'll step you through how to do that now.

1. In the first column, fill in the date of your purchase.
2. In the second column, take note of the payment method (credit card, cash, offset account, and so on; this will help you remember to check all of your accounts for transactions).
3. In the third column, write a short description of your expense (e.g. 'food', 'lunch in the city', 'health insurance').
4. In the 'Category' column, indicate which of the 10 budget categories (from chapter 6) the expense comes under.
5. In the 'Amount' column, enter the exact amount of the expense.

6. The next three columns are key to the process I will outline in chapter 10 about filling out my Monthly Budget worksheet. For now, just know that a 'Direct debit' is any regular bill that is debited from your account each month. If you get one of these, put an 'x' in the 'Direct debit' column. Alternatively, put an 'x' in the column titled 'Future Fund drawdown' if the expense is a drawdown of money from a future fund (I will teach you how to use my Future Fund worksheet in the next chapter to help smooth out large, lumpy expenses over the year). Every other expense gets an 'x' in the 'Variable' column. You should only have one 'x' for each expense.

7. The final column prompts you to consider whether the spending was 'Essential'. Mark it with a Y (yes) or N (no). Make up your own definition of what 'Essential' means to you. It's totally fine—necessary even—to do non-essential spending. But knowing what is essential, and what is more discretionary and could be tightened up if needed, can help you to construct an idea of how big your emergency fund of three to six months of basic living expenses needs to be.

8. The final step to using the Spending Tracker is to highlight each expense using the 10 different-coloured fluoro highlighter pens you designated to the 10 budget categories in chapter 6.

You can ignore the circles at the end of each row for now. They get a satisfying 'tick' at the end of the month once you've transferred all your transactions across to your Monthly Budget worksheet (see chapter 10).

MY SPENDING TRACKER

MONTH   **YEAR**

Date	Payment method	Expense	Category	Amount	Direct debt	Future Fund drawdown	Variable spending	Essential? Y/N	Entered?
				$.					○
				$.					○
				$.					○
				$.					○
				$.					○
				$.					○
				$.					○
				$.					○
				$.					○
				$.					○
				$.					○
				$.					○
				$.					○
				$.					○
				$.					○
				$.					○
				$.					○
				$.					○
				$.					○
				$.					○
				$.					○
				$.					○
				$.					○
				$.					○

Why I track using pen and paper

I get asked a lot why I choose to do this process on paper and by hand. Surely there is an app that I could be using instead? An Excel spreadsheet, at the very least?

In truth, I have a complex 'love–hate' relationship with technology, and my smartphone in particular. I like to disconnect as much as possible. There are just so many distractions on a phone.

I have also found there is magic in the tactile, paper-based system. And science backs me up.

Studies have shown that students retain information better when they record it by hand, rather than electronically. Neuroscientists at the University of Tokyo took 48 students aged between 18 and 29 and had them read a fictional passage about characters discussing an upcoming class schedule. The students were asked to take notes on the details of that schedule for later recall. One-third of the students were asked to take notes by hand using a paper notebook and pen, one-third using a tablet and one-third using a smartphone linked to a keyboard.

The students were then given an hour's break and asked to recall details of the characters' class schedule while in a magnetic resonance imaging (MRI) scanner, which measures blood flow around the brain.

Not only were the students who used the paper-based note-taking system able to recall the information faster, they were more likely to answer questions correctly. The MRI scanner showed significantly increased blood flow around regions of the brain associated with language and visualisation, and in the hippocampus.

Analogue won hands down over digital for memory and recall.

There's also just something so immensely pleasurable about highlighting by hand.

When I post videos online of me methodically highlighting each line in my Spending Tracker, I often get messages to say it induces an 'ASMR' or 'autonomous sensory meridian response' in viewers. I feel it too, when I'm highlighting.

ASMR is a phenomenon whereby people experience relaxation and pleasure—also called 'brain tingles'—from watching videos of people either whispering softly, stroking an object lightly or performing some other repetitive but gentle motion.

In 2018, neuroscientists from the United States stuck another bunch of students in an MRI machine (they do love doing that, don't they?) to measure their brain activity while professing to be experiencing this response. They found significantly heightened activity in the regions of the brain associated with 'reward' and 'emotional arousal'. Interestingly, these are the centres also activated in group 'grooming' activities among primates, inducing a calm state with reduced anxiety and improved mood.

All I can say is, don't knock the old-fashioned way until you've tried it!

Ok, in the next chapter I'm going to tell you all about future funds. I love them so much.

9

Set up Future Funds

When you start tracking your spending, as I have just suggested, you will invariably find you encounter many big expenses which only come up once a quarter, or once a year.

By now you will have gathered that I don't like surprises—especially not big costly bills that lob only occasionally and torpedo my smooth budgeting system.

Future funds are the 'secret sauce' in my monthly budgeting routine to prevent such surprises. I regard establishing future funds as the ultimate act of self-care.

Some people would just call them 'sinking funds'.

But I like to call mine future funds for three reasons.

Firstly, because the overriding goal is to look after Future You.

Secondly, it honours the idea of Australia's longest serving treasurer, Peter Costello, who, in his time, oversaw the establishment of the Australian Government's sovereign wealth fund, called the 'Future Fund'. He also currently chairs it.

Australia's Future Fund was originally set up to cover the future cost of pensions to be paid to retiring public servants. Subsequent governments of both political stripes have so liked the idea that the list of future funds has now grown to also include funding for medical care, disability care, drought and other emergency responses, and Indigenous Australians.

Finally, I just really like alliteration!

How to use the Future Fund worksheets

I use my Future Fund worksheets to smooth out the cost of large bills that hit my bank account through the year with less frequency than monthly, such as utility bills, and also to prepare for large discretionary purchases, such as holidays and gifts.

Expenses to consider setting up a Future Fund for include:

- **things you expect to pay for in a year that are not billed evenly each month (I usually plan in advance by financial year) such as annual and quarterly bills**
- **expenses that are only incurred in certain months of the year—for example, at Christmas time**
- **pleasurable things you want to save up money for throughout the year, such as gifts and holidays**
- **anything lumpy that would blow out your monthly budget.**

At any point in time, I usually have a future fund established to contribute regular monthly amounts to the following costs:

- **Household Future Fund (strata fees, water, council rates, home insurance)**
- **Car Future Fund (rego, insurances, servicing, parts and repairs, roadside assist)**
- **Health Future Fund (annual health insurance premium, gym fees, dental and skin check amounts)**
- **School Future Fund (fees, uniforms and extra-curricular)**
- **Birthdays and Christmas Future Fund (Christmas, birthdays and gifts for friends)**
- **Holidays Future Fund (any domestic and/or overseas holidays I plan during the year).**

And how do I do it?

Get ready for this: it's pretty high tech.

I print out a sheet of paper and write on it. Voilà! A Future Fund!

Here's one of my Future Fund worksheets (you can find a blank version later in this chapter and download as many copies as you like from my website) so you can see this in action. This one is my car Future Fund—if you've got a car, you probably need a car future fund too.

MY  CAR FUTURE FUND

(car, household, holidays, etc)

YEAR _____

EXPENSES

Anticipated annual expense	Estimated cost
registration	$ 400.00
compulsory insurance	$ 450.00
comprehensive insurance	$ 550.00
servicing + repairs	$ 1400.00
parts	$ 1000.00
roadside assist	$ 130.00
	$.
	$.
	$.

Anticipated total annual costs: $ 3930.00

Required monthly contributions: $ 330.00

DRAWDOWNS

Date	Expense	Amount	Tally
26/10	battery	$ 428.00	$ 428.00
23/11	service + repair	$ 660.07	$ 1088.00
25/11	compuls. ins.	$ 437.91	$ 1525.98
25/11	rego	$ 381.00	$ 1906.98
10/1	roadside	$ 132.00	$ 2038.98
		$.	$.
		$.	$.
		$.	$.
		$.	$.
		$.	$.
		$.	$.
		$.	$.
		$.	$.
		$.	$.
		$.	$.
		$.	$.
		$.	$.
		$.	$.
		$.	$.
		$.	$.
		$.	$.
		$.	$.
		$.	$.
		$.	$.
		$.	$.

Annual drawdowns total: $.

CONTRIBUTIONS

J	A	S	O	N	D	J	F	M	A	M	J

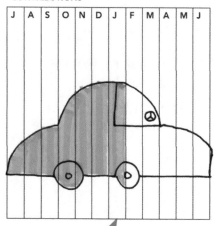

Please take a moment
to enjoy my highly developed
artistic skills ☺ Brrum brrum!

Before the start of each financial year, I sit down and plan out my future funds.

For each one, I list all the anticipated annual expenses I expect to incur—expenses that my monthly budget would otherwise fail to capture.

EXPENSES

Anticipated annual expense	Estimated cost
registration	$ 400 . 00
compulsory insurance	$ 450 . 00
comprehensive insurance	$ 550 . 00
servicing + repairs	$ 1400 . 00
parts	$ 1000 . 00
roadside assist	$ 130 . 00
	$.
	$.
Anticipated total annual costs:	$ 3930 . 00
Required monthly contributions:	$ 330 . 00

I then tally up the total cost (and enter this figure under 'Anticipated total annual cost') and divide it by 12 to get a figure for 'Required monthly contributions'.

Next, I expertly draw a pretty picture in the bottom left-hand box, which I shade in by column at the end of every month that I have set money aside for it. As I said, high tech. Here's an example of one of mine:

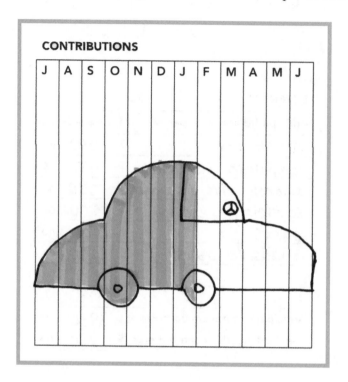

CONTRIBUTIONS

J	A	S	O	N	D	J	F	M	A	M	J

I like to set these up before the start of every financial year, hence why my columns are labeled 'J' for July, through to 'J' for June'.

But you can really start them any time you like. Just choose the number of months over which you would like to smooth the cost and divide the cost by that number of months — for example, if there are 10 months remaining of the current financial year, you would divide the cost by 10 to get the monthly contribution amount.

Throughout the year, at the end of each month, I also record in the right-hand column any drawdowns from the fund—that is, times when I've spent money earmarked to be covered by the fund.

These have been marked on my Spending Tracker with an 'x' under the column 'Future Fund drawdown'. Once these expenses have also been recorded as drawdowns on the relevant Future Fund worksheet, they get a 'tick' in the 'entered' column on my Spending Tracker.

DRAWDOWNS

Date	Expense	Amount	Tally
26/10	battery	$ 428 . 00	$ 428 .00
23/11	service + repair	$ 660 . 07	$ 1088 . 00
25/11	compuls. ins.	$ 437 . 91	$ 1525 . 98
25/11	rego	$ 381 . 00	$ 1906 . 98
10/1	roadside	$ 132 . 00	$ 2038 . 98
		$.	$.
		$.	$.
		$.	$.
		$.	$.
		$.	$.

Crucially, lumpy drawdowns don't affect my monthly bottom line. Only my smoothed out monthly fund contributions get counted as an expense on my Monthly Budget worksheet (which we're about to get to in Chapter 10). That's kind of the whole point!

At the end of the year, I tally the drawdowns on my Future Fund worksheets to see if I managed to set aside enough money via my monthly contributions to cover my anticipated total annual costs.

It's not unusual for them to be a bit off. In this case, money can be pulled from unspent money in other future funds or taken out of my surplus for whatever is the final month of the year (for me, this is June because I create my future funds to span the financial year from July to June). If I have surplus funds, I put them to work by either paying off some more debt or investing.

A common question I'm asked is, 'Jess, what if a big expense hits early in the year?'

I am fortunate in that I have a substantial buffer sitting in my main transaction account. Should a large expense fall due early in the financial year, before my contributions have time to build up to cover it, they eat into this buffer. I know that by the end of the financial year, it will be fully restocked by contributions to cover the expense.

If funds are tighter for you, or you knew, for example, that you were planning to embark on a big holiday on the first of July, you would probably need to start saving for that in the year prior.

Here is a blank worksheet for you to photocopy, or fill in here, to try your hand at creating a completed Future Fund worksheet. Just follow the steps below to complete a worksheet for each of your future funds. You'll need a separate sheet for each future fund you want to establish. You can download more copies from my website, jessicairvine.com.au. Print off as many as you like!

MY _____ FUTURE FUND
(car, household, holidays, etc)

YEAR _____

EXPENSES

Anticipated annual expense	Estimated cost
	$.
	$.
	$.
	$.
	$.
	$.
	$.
	$.
Anticipated total annual costs:	$.
Required monthly contributions:	$.

CONTRIBUTIONS

J	A	S	O	N	D	J	F	M	A	M	J

DRAWDOWNS

Date	Expense	Amount	Tally
		$.	$.
		$.	$.
		$.	$.
		$.	$.
		$.	$.
		$.	$.
		$.	$.
		$.	$.
		$.	$.
		$.	$.
		$.	$.
		$.	$.
		$.	$.
		$.	$.
		$.	$.
		$.	$.
		$.	$.
		$.	$.
		$.	$.
		$.	$.
		$.	$.
		$.	$.
		$.	$.
		$.	$.
		$.	$.
		$.	$.
Annual drawdowns total:			$.

How to create your Future Funds

Here's a step-by-step guide for creating a Future Fund.

1. Print out the Future Fund worksheet and write the name and year of your fund at the top.

2. Try not to have too many funds to avoid things becoming unwieldy. You can have separate funds for different expenses in the same category (holidays, birthdays, etc.) or you can bunch all those expenses under a category name (utilities, household, etc.).

3. Look over your expenses for the categories you completed in part II.

4. For each category that has one or more large expenses that fall outside a regular monthly billing schedule:
   - list each expense under 'Anticipated annual expense' on the worksheet for that category
   - write the estimated annual cost for each expense
   - write the total of the estimated costs under 'Anticipated total annual cost'.

5. Divide the total annual cost by 12 and write the amount under 'Required monthly contributions'.

6. Draw a pretty picture to represent your fund in the box provided on the Future Fund worksheet. Each month, colour a bar in using the highlighter that corresponds to that category.

How to maintain your Future Funds

Keeping track of your future funds involves just a few steps.

1. When recording future fund expenses on your Spending Tracker, mark an 'x' in the column titled 'Future Fund drawdowns' to denote a drawdown for an expense covered by a fund.

2. At the end of each month, scan your Spending Tracker for future fund drawdowns and transfer the information across to the right-hand side of the relevant Future Fund worksheet. You get to put a 'tick' in the circle on the Spending Tracker next to every expense you successfully migrate across.

3. I like to keep a running tally on my Future Fund worksheets in the final column provided, so I can see at the end of each month how much of my total allocated funds have already been spent.

4. At the end of the final month of the year, your drawdown tally column should show the total amount you *actually* spent. You can record this in the final space for 'Annual drawdowns'.

Of course, if you like having multiple bank accounts (I don't, for reasons I'll address in chapter 11), you could always set up separate accounts for each Future Fund you decide to establish.

You could set up monthly automatic transfers from your main account into your Future Fund accounts at the level of your calculated monthly contributions. If you did this, of course, you would have to wait until you had enough money in the actual accounts before spending money from them.

Either way, if you discover you're heading towards a large unanticipated expense, you can always increase your contributions for the rest of the year. Or you may choose to reduce the number of drawdowns from a more discretionary fund such as 'Lifestyle'. For true emergencies, you should always have an emergency fund available.

Here's the thing about future funds. It's likely they'll be a bit off. Expenses may be bigger or smaller than anticipated. That's okay. The important thing is that you take a stab at anticipating them. You will feel so much more in control, and Future You will thank you, I promise.

10

Check in with your budget each month

The last day of the month is always my favourite day of the month. Why? Because it's the day I sit down to take a look at where all my money went for the month and see what I have left over to invest. I do this using my Monthly Budget worksheet, which you'll find below. It's also available for download for free from my website, jessicairvine.com.au.

The worksheet is designed to give you an overall snapshot of your income, expenses and resulting surplus or deficit for the month, which will help to guide your regular investment decisions. If you do it 12 months in a row, of course, you'll have a complete annual picture that you can also use to inform your Annual Budget.

How to use the Monthly Budget worksheet

You'll see that the structure of my Monthly Budget worksheet roughly follows the first three of the four steps to financial freedom I outlined in part I, namely: earn, spend and create a surplus. We'll deal with the fourth step—'Putting your surplus to work'—a bit later on. On the next page is a blank worksheet and next to it is one I've completed, to give you an idea of what you're shooting for. Don't worry, we'll take each section in turn—just follow the eight steps that follow.

MY MONTHLY BUDGET

MONTH _____ YEAR _____

INCOME			
	$.		$.
	$.		$.

EXPENSES	

Direct debits	Amount
	$.
	$.
	$.
	$.
	$.
	$.
Total direct debits	$.

Variable spending	Amount
	$.
	$.
	$.
	$.
	$.
	$.
	$.
	$.
	$.
	$.
	$.
	$.
	$.
	$.
Total variable spending	$.

Future Fund contributions	Amount
	$.
	$.
	$.
	$.
	$.
	$.
Total Future Fund contributions	$.

TOTAL INCOME $.

TOTAL EXPENSES $.

SURPLUS $.

What I did well …

_____

Something to improve …

_____

MY MONTHLY BUDGET

MONTH __JANUARY__   YEAR _____

INCOME			
Salary	$.	Dividends	$
Sole trader income	$.	Facebook marketplace sale	$

EXPENSES

Direct debits	Amount	Variable spending		Amount
mortgage minimum repay	$ 2599.00	HOUSEHOLD · decor		$ 73.94
electricity	$ 112.35	· cleaning		$ 25.57
internet	$ 59.95	· hygiene		$ 7.99
cloud storage	$ 4.49	TRANSPORT · petrol		$ 84.68
Netflix	$ 10.99	FOOD		$ 547.85
union fees	$ 58.04	HEALTH · drs + specialists		$ 80.45
Total direct debits	$ 2844.82	· medicine		$ 25.25
		· fitness		$ 26.50

Future Fund contributions	Amount			
HOUSEHOLD	$ 825.00	EDUCATION · books		$ 9.99
CAR	$ 330.00	· stationery		$ 4.98
HEALTH	$ 545.00	APPEARANCE · accessories		$ 19.95
SCHOOL	$ 920.00	LIFESTYLE · eating out		$ 205.97
BIRTHDAYS + XMAS	$ 85.00	· alcohol		$ 15.38
HOLIDAYS	$ 485.00	· hobbies		$ 52.93
Total Future Fund contributions	$ 3190.00	PROFESSIONAL FEES · pocket money		$ 50.00
		Total variable spending		$ 1231.43

TOTAL INCOME $.

TOTAL EXPENSES $ 7266.25

SURPLUS $.

What I did well...
sold old toys on facebook

Something to improve...
food spend has crept up...

The full A4 downloadable version of this
worksheet on my website jessicairvine.com.au
has extra spaces, for just that reason!

1. Identify all your income

Write your monthly disposable income from all sources (as discussed for annual income in chapter 7) in the first box provided under 'Income'.

INCOME			
	$.		$.
	$.		$.

Now add up all your income sources and write your 'Total income' at the bottom of the worksheet in the space provided.

2. Identify your monthly direct debits

Now it's time to sort your expenses. I start by listing all my monthly direct debits. These are the monthly amounts I've granted organisations explicit permission to charge me for automatically each month.

Direct debits	Amount
	$.
	$.
	$.
	$.
	$.
	$.
	$.
	$.
	$.
	$.
Total direct debits	$.

Where possible, I try to pay my bills monthly. It's not always possible, however, and I don't do it in cases where it's cheaper to pay quarterly or annually in advance. Always do the maths on the cheapest overall billing option you are given.

To identify monthly bills, use the information from your Spending Tracker. Run your eye down the sheet for any 'x's marked in the 'Direct debit' column on the tracker. Once you've transferred your direct debit amounts from the Spending Tracker to the Monthly Budget worksheet, give those lines on the Spending Tracker a tick in the circle at the end of each row, under the heading 'Entered?' Truly, this is so satisfying!

Common monthly direct debits include electricity bills, TV streaming subscriptions, gym fees, cloud storage fees, union fees, mortgage interest and rent.

I like listing these out separately on my worksheet as it can remind me to cancel unused subscriptions or shop around for better deals. Don't set and forget your direct debits!

3. List your Future Fund contributions

You can find your future fund monthly contribution amounts on the individual Future Fund worksheets we set up in the previous chapter. These amounts are fixed monthly and shouldn't change throughout the year. That's the magic! You've smoothed out all those lumpy expenses into a neat monthly figure to ensure your monthly budget isn't torpedoed by big irregular expenses. Well done you!

Simply list your monthly contribution amounts in the following box, along with a monthly total.

Future Fund contributions	Amount
	$.
	$.
	$.
	$.
	$.
	$.
	$.
	$.
	$.
	$.
Total Future Fund contributions	$.

Remember at the end of each month to also record all your drawdowns from your future funds — denoted by an 'x' on your Spending Tracker — on your individual Future Fund worksheets in the box provided for this. Once you have done this, you can also put a 'tick' at the end of these expenses on your Spending Tracker and shade in a column on all your Future Fund worksheet pictures to show you have made the monthly contribution for that month.

4. List all your 'variable' spending by category

Okay, so you're abreast of your monthly direct debits and you've listed your monthly future fund contributions.

The rest of your spending goes under 'Variable spending'.

Variable spending comprises all the day-to-day regular and ad hoc purchases we make such as food, bus trips, petrol, tolls, medicines, food, books, eating out and movie tickets. In other words, whatever else hits your account that you haven't already accounted for. You can see my regular items on my example Monthly Budget worksheet on page 227.

I group expenses by category and subcategory in this box.

Variable spending	Amount
HOUSEHOLD · decor	$ 73 . 94
· cleaning	$ 25 . 57
· hygiene	$ 7 . 99
TRANSPORT · petrol	$ 84 . 68
FOOD	$ 547 . 85
HEALTH · drs + specialists	$ 80 . 45
· medicine	$ 25 . 25
· fitness	$ 26 . 50
EDUCATION · books	$ 9 . 99
· stationery	$ 4 . 98
APPEARANCE · accessories	$ 19 . 95
LIFESTYLE · eating out	$ 205 . 97
· alcohol	$ 15 . 38
· hobbies	$ 52 . 93
PROFESSIONAL FEES · pocket money	$ 50 . 00
Total variable spending	$ 1231 . 43

I do this by running my eye down my completed Spending Tracker for the month and looking for expenses of the same colour.

I start with 'Household' (Housing is usually a direct debt expense for most people) and then move to 'Utilities', 'Transport', and so on. You could choose to just tally a total amount for each of the 10 major budget categories, but I like to list out my main regular subcategories too, like 'decor' and 'eating out'. Once I've added up all variable expenses for a certain category, I put a 'tick' on my Spending Tracker in the circle at the end of each expense to indicate that I have counted it.

If you're really looking to boost your savings for the month, variable spending is an area where you can try to tighten things up.

Your direct debits and future fund contributions are like putting your big rocks in the jar first. Then you can fill your spending with as many little pebbles as you can fit, depending on how much you want to save.

5. Add up all your spending

Once every row on your Spending Tracker has a tick, you will know that all your monthly spending transactions have been transferred to your Monthly Budget and it is complete.

The next bit's pretty simple: add up the totals on your Monthly Budget for 'Direct debits', 'Future Fund contributions' and 'Variable spending'.

Then add all those together to get your 'Total expenses' figure for the month, which you record beneath your 'Total income' figure at the bottom of the template.

6. Calculate your monthly surplus

Now it's time to unleash your inner mathematician by subtracting your total expenses from your total income.

I told you that you have all the necessary maths skills, didn't I?

Then write the dollar figure in the box for 'Surplus'.

I have exercised the power of positive thinking here, and assumed you will be in surplus. If your number is negative, of course, you're in deficit. Just record it with a 'negative' sign in front.

So, how did you do? Did you manage to get a monthly surplus?

If you've ended up with a negative surplus number for the month, don't worry. At least you know where you stand. Look back over chapters 6 and 7 to see if you can't find some bills to slash or ways to boost your income.

If you've generated a surplus, it's time to decide what to do with it.

7. Put your surplus to work

Provided you're still with me and you have a surplus to work with, here is the hierarchy of potential jobs I'd like you to consider for your surplus:

1. Make sure you have an emergency fund of easily accessible savings — aim for $1000 as a bare minimum. This is to make sure you don't have to go into debt to pay for any surprise expenses that may still arise.
2. Decide what voluntary payments you wish to make to pay down your debts. Prioritise paying down high interest debt first.
3. Top up your emergency fund if it is not fully stocked to three or six months of basic living expenses (remember you get to choose how much lets you sleep at night).
4. Consider setting money aside for any long-term, multi-year savings goals you have, such as a first home deposit, major home renovations, wedding or buying a new car.
5. Consider whether you have made the most out of the tax concessions available on money socked away in super. (I outlined this in chapter 7.) If not, consider a contribution.
6. If, and only if, you have done all these things, congratulations! You get to invest!

INVESTING IN SHARES

Any investing is best done only once you're confident you don't need to access this money in the short term. Investing in shares should always be for the longer term and involves more risk, including greater volatility in the value of your assets. You don't want to have to dip into your investments to fund your current consumption.

But if you're following all these monthly steps, it is certainly something to consider. Over the longer term, it's a great way to both protect your savings from inflation and grow your wealth. Of course, there are many other ways you could considering deploying your surplus, including using the money to invest in other assets, or to cover the borrowing costs on an investment loan for property or shares.

Personally, I currently make a habit at the end of the month of transferring my surplus straight into my share brokerage account and executing a trade when it lands.

I can do this confidently because I know I have paid off any high interest debt, saved an emergency fund, bought a home to live in and maxxed out my annual concessionary contributions to super. I'm confident I don't need to access the money I invest for 10 to 20 years. I may, in the future, decide to deploy some of my surplus in other ways, such as covering the costs of an investment loan, but I haven't got there yet.

Then it becomes a fun game to see how big a surplus I can come up with each month to look after Future Jess, while also letting Today Jess live a little.

I invest mainly in low-cost 'indexed' funds, which track a broad index such as the ASX 200 or the top global companies. I access them by buying units in an Exchange Traded Fund (ETF), which you can buy just as you would any other individual shares, by opening a brokerage account and executing a trade.

Not all ETFs are created equal and some are much riskier and high cost than others. You must do your own individual research if you are looking to invest in shares for a strategy that matches your risk appetite. But low-cost, broad-index tracking ETFs are a great place to begin your investing journey.

There's probably another book in that, actually …

8. Make your own budget binder!

All right, if you've made it this far and you're a paper-based tracker like me, you're going to need a central place to house all your worksheets.

I have a basic white binder, with divider tabs by financial year. Here's a picture:

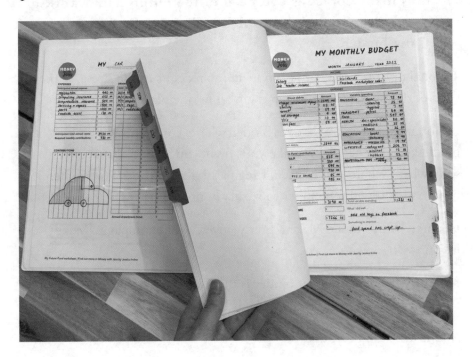

Here's what you'll need to make an identical budget binder to neatly store all your resources for one year:

- **12 divider tabs: one for each month of the year (I bought my dividers from Officeworks and they arrange the months by financial year July to June)**
- **12 copies of my Monthly Budget worksheet: one to sit behind each monthly divider**
- **24 printed copies of my Spending Tracker: I generally find I use about two per month and I print extras later if needed**
- **as many copies as you need of the Future Fund worksheet (usually about eight), which I slip into the front pocket of my binder.**

Throughout the month, I also pop all my receipts in the sleeve at the back of the binder, just to keep them all in one place.

Importantly, I keep my budget binder where it is highly visible on my desk. If you decide to make your own, you should also keep it somewhere where you can see it regularly, like your desk or kitchen bench, so you will remember to regularly update it.

Decorate your binder. Make a pretty cover. Add extra pages. Make it your own.

I firmly believe my budget binder is the foundation stone upon which every good money decision I make is built.

And now it can be yours, too.

11

Q&A with Jess

Now I'm sure you have lots of questions, so let me answer a few commonly asked ones for you.

How long does this all take?

To be honest, it depends. It certainly takes longer at the start while you wrap your head around everything. I generally update my Spending Tracker about once or twice a week, which takes 15 minutes or so.

It also takes me about half an hour to an hour at the end of each month to fill out my Monthly Budget worksheet and update my Future Fund worksheets.

For the same time it takes to watch a movie, it's well worth the effort, I'd say.

How do you structure your bank accounts?

I have just one bank account—an offset account against my mortgage—where I stash my emergency funds. All my pay goes into that account. All my direct debits are paid out of it.

I used to have a credit card, but I cut it up because it was easier to have only one account to scan for expenses. Also, when banks assess how much you can borrow, they assume you have to pay interest on your full credit card limit. So even if you pay it off every month, and pay no interest, they have to assume you could use it to the max, and this reduces your borrowing capacity.

I also tend to be a cashless spender because this makes it easier to keep track of transactions.

Why don't you set up multiple bank accounts for your future funds?

Mainly because I don't need to. I have a significant buffer in my main transaction account and my paper-based worksheets let me know exactly how I'm tracking.

I also think multiple accounts lock you into staying with your current bank or lender. Once you've been through the laborious process of establishing multiple accounts, it's only natural you'll be reluctant to have to do it all again with another financial institution.

I put a high value on remaining nimble and independent so I can switch banks whenever I like for a better deal—something I do regularly!

Why don't you like the 50:30:20 budgeting rule?

This is the rule that says to allocate 50 per cent of your income to needs, 30 per cent to wants and 20 per cent to savings.

Following this rule, if Person A is on an income of say $50 000, they would have to put aside $25 000 for bills and necessities. Person B on an income of $200 000 would set aside $100 000 for such necessities. But would Person B's necessities really cost four times as much as Person A's?

Similarly, with the '30 per cent for fun' money, Person A gets $15 000 to play with, but Person B basically expects to blow $60 000 a year. Perhaps Person B might be better off saving more and retiring early?

It's just too much of a 'one-size-fits-all' solution to me.

Of course, if it works for you, you do you! You can still use my system to track and see where your money is going and to check whether you're on course with your pre-determined percentages.

Why don't you use 'buckets'?

Again, if you have an existing buckets system that works for you, that's great! I prefer to have a more nuanced understanding of where my money goes than the bucket system allows for.

Yes, this might be more laborious (though not onerously so, I'd say) but that's actually the point. I am on a mission to slow down and really examine my spending to become more deliberate with my money choices.

I'm also not a fan of setting up multiple bank accounts, as I've mentioned.

Are there any budgeting apps you recommend?

I get asked this a lot. And the honest answer is 'no'. I've yet to find one that sensibly captures everything I want it to. I also don't want to effectively outsource my budgeting system to an app that may either rise in price, cease to exist or tinker with its system in ways I don't like.

I have tried a few. But I usually find them clunky or they don't draw or correctly label the information transfers from my bank account.

That's why I wrote this book.

Do I have to do the Future Funds thing?

I get it: it's a lot. If you have a big enough cash savings buffer for meeting any big expenses that might lob, such as a $2000 quarterly strata bill, you could just track your direct debits and everything else under 'Variable spending' in your Monthly Budget.

It will mean your monthly surpluses will swing more wildly and perhaps some months will be negative. You can always establish funds at a later point if you do find you want to smooth out your monthly savings figure.

Can I steal your categories and keep going with my own budgeting structure?

Yes, of course you can. If you already have a system that keeps you abreast of your expenses and your income, and you regularly put your savings to work by paying off debt or investing, I am happy for you! Keep going! I hope you got value out of my book by perhaps checking off a few other expenses to consider for your budget or by giving some of my savings hacks a go. ☺

Can you help get my partner on board to follow your method?

Short answer: no. I'm not currently offering couples counselling, and given my track record, you wouldn't want it if I did! Haha.

I believe my system can work for individuals and households. If one person is happy to delegate, the other person—the more enthusiastic tracker—could track all the household income and spending. Perhaps the less enthused partner could be allocated a monthly sum to spend on 'lifestyle' and then report back how much was spent over the month.

I do think it is important to come together at the end of the month to agree on what to do with any savings—whether to pay off debt or invest, and so on. That's the fun part, after all! If the more reluctant partner gets to be an active participant in deciding where the money is invested, maybe that will help to engage them in the process. Couples operating this way would do well to have shared access accounts and to do mostly cashless spending.

If you really can't agree, that could be a red flag for your relationship and you might want to seek counselling to discuss it. Given the central role of having a sense of 'financial control' in a person's wellbeing, I think you do need to discuss that. But as I say, I'm not a licensed therapist.

What about spending that spans multiple categories or has multiple purposes?

That's like asking, is a mountain bike really for transport or recreation? Are laptops for education or for gaming?

Inevitably, there will be some items that potentially fall under several of my budget categories—although I really have tried to avoid this as much as possible!

In such cases, I defer to the United Nations (as one always must, surely?): 'The general rule followed has been to assign multi-purpose goods and services to the division that represents the predominant purpose'. Just pick the category that makes the most intuitive sense to you and—importantly—stick with it.

What about delivery charges and tips?

Incorporate this expense into the cost of whatever you bought and had delivered, or the service performed. If you tip a waiter or Uber Eats driver, include it in the cost of your meal. If you tip a hairdresser, include it in the cost of your hair cut.

12

Next steps

At its heart, budgeting is, I believe, about being able to decide if your current spending is in alignment with your values. It's also about paying attention to what brings you pleasure and deciding if you're taking good enough care of Future You. And, if not, taking action to change that.

Knowing your personal numbers for how much you currently spend and how much you want to spend in the future unlocks the answers to a host of common questions, such as how much you can afford to borrow, how big a savings reserve you need, whether you can walk away from a job you hate and how much you need in retirement.

It's the secret to gaining financial control of your life, which leads to better self-esteem, personal confidence and a sense of ease and calm.

Sure, wealth creation is the by-product of that. But the true treasure in budgeting lies, I believe, in the process—not the outcome. The sense of peace and calm that descends when you know you are living within your means and planning the steps towards the life you dream of—that's the real magic, not getting rich. Once you have that control and sense of inner calm, you are truly wealthy. The money's just a bonus.

Staying on track

You know by now how much I love a listicle, so here is a parting one. These are a few ways to keep you on track with your budgeting journey.

1. **Keep tracking your spending.** I truly believe this is the most insightful thing you can do on an ongoing basis to become more mindful of your money habits. I adore my Spending Tracker and my manual process for writing out my expenses and then highlighting them. It relaxes me. I recognise this might not be for everyone on an ongoing basis. But do at least give it a try.

2. **Start small.** Choose one savings hack you can work on and do it this week. Then next week, pick another. Small steps build to big change over time.

3. **Ditch 'should' for 'could'.** Whenever you find yourself stressing about a 'should' question, replace it with 'could'. If you find yourself worrying about whether you *should* rent or buy a home, reframe it as, 'I *could* either rent or buy my home: both are options available to me, depending on my preferences'. Similarly, people often worry about whether they *should* invest in shares or property. Reframe it as, 'I *could* invest in either shares or property, depending on my preferences and goals'. This simple switch can bring you back to a mindset of the opportunities that are open to you in life, rather than getting stuck on trying to find a perfect solution. There is no one-size-fits-all, remember?

4. **Try an 'elimination diet' for your spending.** Nutritionists advise to give up certain things to see if you notice a change. I think it's helpful to go without certain things in your budget to see if you miss them. Here are some things I have tried giving up at times: alcohol, haircuts and dyeing hair, Netflix, gym fees, buying clothes, expensive shampoos and makeup. I ended up rejoining the gym, and

I still have the occasional social drink, but each experiment honed the sense of joy I now have when I do spend money on those things. (I haven't had a professional haircut in years.)

5. **Ask yourself: 'If not the cheapest, why not?'** Advertising is designed to convince us we need fancier versions of the same product. I like to try to undo that by trying the cheapest version first, and then working my way up. Things I have tried the cheapest of are toothpaste, shampoo, conditioner and mascara. Of course, you may have non-monetary reasons to want a more expensive version, such as concern about the environment. If so, you can opt for the lowest priced eco-friendly option.

6. **When shopping, remember my 'Four S's for Saving'.** They are:

   - *second hand:* see if you can get the product second hand instead
   - *shop around:* always shop around to get the best price
   - *consider sharing:* do you actually need to buy it or can you rent it or share it with someone you know?
   - *sleep on it:* if you still want it after a certain period, fine. But often you get the best discounts (or save yourself a lot of money by not buying) when you're willing to walk away and sleep on it.

7. **Keep checking in with your emotions and what thoughts might be causing them.** You won't always be happy and you won't always be motivated to track your spending. And that's okay. Refer to my emotions wheel on page 8 as often as you need to and try to identify the thoughts underlying your emotions.

8. **Take a break if you need to.** There is a balance to be struck between awareness and obsessive control. Beginning to take control of your finances can be overwhelming at first. Have compassion for yourself if you drop off. Focus on how far you've come.

9. **Keep in touch.** You can follow me on Instagram, @moneywithjess, or head to my website, jessicairvine.com.au, to continue the conversation. I look forward to seeing you there.

I'm so excited to have hopefully been there with you when you started out on your budgeting journey, or perhaps to have helped you refine your existing budget.

Keep up the great work!

A final note

One weekday evening, about a week before this manuscript was due to my publisher, I was cooking dinner in the kitchen while my son played an online game in the living room of our flat.

'Mum, come!', he cried out to me in the somewhat imperious manner he's developed lately and I've been trying to train him out of.

'How can you say that more politely?' I hollered back from the kitchen.

'Mum, can you come?' he replied, with the same efficiency with words that often makes me chuckle, as it did that night as I wandered into the living room to stand beside him at the laptop.

'Can I buy this?' he asked.

'What is it?' I replied, before he explained he'd like to spend $28.99 to unlock access to a VIP area in an online game.

I immediately expressed my strong belief that this would, indeed, be a very silly way to spend money.

We quibbled briefly before I remembered my get-out-of-jail-free card, which I developed specifically for getting out of just such occasions.

'Well, you know, you always have your budget to spend, darling,' I said.

For the past year or so, I have been setting him a monthly budget of $50 to spend as he sees fit. We keep track of his purchases on a little printable sheet I've made up. There are 50 circles and we colour one in — in highlighter, of course — for every dollar he decides to spend. When the circles are filled, he has to wait until the next month for his budget to 'recharge'.

I'd like to say I designed this system as an ingenious, evidence-based early financial literacy intervention measure. In all honestly, it was just born more of a desire to spare myself exactly the sort of endless exchanges we were presently engaged in.

As an aside — the relevance of which will soon become apparent — I've also always drilled into him from an early age the importance of body autonomy and how you get to decide who touches your body. 'My body, my choice,' was the mantra I'd been educating him with.

It must have stuck.

Because, as we bickered further over the in-game purchase, our argument reached a sudden crescendo when he yelled out, with trademark word efficiency: 'My money, my choice!'

'My money, my choice', he repeated.

At which point, I crumpled and smiled.

My money, my choice.

Well, I'll be!

I'd just spent the better part of a year devoting my evenings, weekends and an entire year's worth of annual leave — not to mention considerable shower thinking time — to composing a lengthy manuscript about how to manage your money.

And my seven-year-old son had just summed up my central message in four words:

My money, my choice.

Your money, your choice.

I smiled because his simple phrase made me realise just how far I've come in my own journey with money. All the work I've done to transform my attitude towards money from one of despair and disempowerment, to one of feeling completely and powerfully in charge of where my money goes.

And I smiled because, on the available evidence, I'm doing my job of passing on that precious knowledge to the next generation.

I hope I have now, through this book, been able to pass on some of this knowledge to you, too.

For those of you who have read this far, first of all: thank you. Writing this has been one of the most challenging and rewarding experiences of my life. I set out to explain in detail the budgeting system I've used to turn my financial life around; the system I built that has brought me — and continues to bring me — immense calm and joy on a daily basis.

My aim is to share that feeling with as many people as possible. I sincerely hope you're feeling more inspired to stay on top of your finances a bit better or at least to try a few of the savings hacks I've mentioned.

But if you end up remembering only one thing from this book, let it be that phrase — from the mouth of my babe — 'Your money, your choice'.

You get to choose how you spend your money, and through those decisions, how you spend your life.

Figure out the things you enjoy doing in life and do them—both now, and in the future. It's as simple—and as challenging—as that.

Only you can ever truly know what brings you joy. Perhaps you haven't really discovered it yet. But over time—perhaps with some considerable trial and error, as most of us experience—I believe you will.

Once you pay close enough attention, I believe you'll find that joy is yours for the choosing.

I wish you all the joy in the world.

Take care,

Jess xx

Index